Around the World in Eighty Days

A musical

Book, Music and Lyrics by Phil Willmott

Additional music and arrangements
by Annemarie Lewis Thomas

Freely adapted from the novel by Jules Verne

Samuel French — London
New York - Toronto - Hollywood

SAMUEL FRENCH LTD, 52 FITZROY STREET, LONDON W1T 5JR, or their authorized agents, issue licences to amateurs to give performances of this play on payment of a fee. This fee is subject to contract and subject to variation at the sole discretion of Samuel French Ltd.

Licences for amateur performances are issued subject to the understanding that it shall be made clear in all advertising matter that the audience will witness an amateur performance; that the names of the authors of the plays shall be included on all programmes; and that the integrity of the authors' work will be preserved.

The publication of this play does not imply that it is necessarily available for performance by amateurs or professionals, either in the British Isles or Overseas. Amateurs and professionals considering a production are strongly advised in their own interests to apply to the appropriate agents for written consent before starting rehearsals or booking a theatre or hall.

The Professional Repertory Rights are controlled by SAMUEL FRENCH LTD. The Professional Rights, other than Repertory Rights, are controlled by CURTIS BROWN LTD, 4th Floor, Haymarket House, 28/29 Haymarket, London SW1Y 4SP.

ISBN 0 573 08120 4

AROUND THE WORLD IN EIGHTY DAYS

Originally commissioned and produced by Caroline Routh
for Tom Morris and Battersea Arts Centre, London, on
30th November 2001, with the following cast:

Jean Passepartout	Timothy Mitchell
Phileas Fogg	Bill Ward
Princess Auoda	Rae Baker
Captain Fix	Phil Willmott
Miss Fotherington	Jane Lucas
Katy O'Flathery	Chevaun Marsh
Hitch — A Mormon Preacher	Simon Greenhill
Queen Victoria	Shirley Barr
Prime Minister Disraeli	Alan Atkins
Sherlock Holmes	Nick Smithers
Barnum	Nick Smithers
Dr Watson	Paul Oliver
Jessie James	Paul Oliver

The Rest of the world played by Ed Jaspers, Angela
Michaels, Sarah Ratheram, Joseph Wicks, Jordan Saflor,
Amy Ip, Natalie Tapper, Emma Thornett, Stephanie
Tavernier, Sarah Lawn, Holly Boothby, Chantal Bell

Directed by Phil Willmott with Catriona McLaughlin
Musical direction by Annemarie Lewis Thomas
Choreographed by Jack Gunn
Set and lighting designed by Hansjorg Schmidt
Costume designed by Andri Korniotis
Puppet design and direction by Mervyn Millar
Sound designed by Adam Keeper

CHARACTERS

This show was originally performed by a cast of twenty-three but would easily be presented with half that number if the actors double.

The Mayor
Citizens of Greenwich
Journalists
Phileas Fogg
Passepartout
Captain James Fix
The Master of Ceremonies: at the Moulin Rose, Paris
Katy O'Flathery: a cabaret singer
Helga
Sheila
Yuki
Trudy } Katy's international all-girl revue
Pam
Svetlana
Morag
Kitchen and Waiting staff: at The Moulin Rose
A Parisian Station Porter
Queen Victoria
Prime Minister Disraeli
Sherlock Holmes
Dr Watson
Dr Livingstone
Stanley, his friend
The Concierge: at the Bombay Hilton
Princess Aouda
Two Ticket Collectors: on the India Railway
Eugene: an elephant
Indian Priests
Funeral Dancers
Chinese Dragon Dancers
Miss Fotherington: a missionary
A Circus Barker
Interpreter: of the Circus Barker
Mrs Chang: an opium seller

Opium Dealers
Phineas T. Barnum: a circus proprietor
Jesse James: an outlaw
James's Gang
A Wild West Saloon Hostess
Tammy Lou
Tammy Lou's All Girl USA revue
Guard: on the Union Pacific railroad
Hitch: Mormon polygamist
Hitch's Mormon wives
A Cowardly Porter
A Liverpudlian Detective
A Liverpudlian Policeman
A Sailor's Wife
Other Sailors and their Wives

The action takes place at various stops around the world

Time — 1873

MUSICAL NUMBERS

ACT I

No. 1	**Overture/Eighty Days**	Company
No. 2	**Around the World With Katy's Girls**	Katy and Her Girls
No. 3	**Passepartout**	Passepartout, Katy and Company
No. 5	**The Maharaja's Child**	Aouda
No. 6	**Bang!**	Captain Fix
No. 7	**Jungle Honeymoon**	Passepartout, Fogg
No. 8	**The Nizam**	Company
No. 9	**Passepartout — Reprise**	Passepartout and Company

ACT II

No. 11	**Sorry Dragon**	Passepartout and Aouda
No. 12	**The Luxuriant Brew**	Captain Fix, Mrs Chang and Opium Dealers
No. 12b	**The Water is Wide** (traditional)	Sailors
No.13	**What Do I Love?**	Fogg and Aouda
No. 14	**Jungle Honeymoon — Reprise**	Passepartout
No. 16	**Around the States with Tammy's Dames**	Tammy Lou and Show Girls
No. 17	**Life Here in the Wilderness**	Hitch and Wives
No. 20	**How Was I to Know/The Water is Wide**	Aouda and Company
No. 21	**Finale (Passepartout)**	Company
No. 22	**Bows and Finale**	Company

Vocal score and bandparts are available on hire from Samuel French Ltd

PRODUCTION NOTES

In the original London production the theatre environment was transformed into a huge railway station lost property and left luggage office. There were stacks of trunks, suitcases, umbrellas and junk piled high. The colours were predominately warm and sepia. By contrast, the many props, puppets, bits of scenery and sometimes actors who emerged from this luggage were brightly coloured.

In the spectacular Liverpool Playhouse Production the stage looked like the inside of a giant Victorian pocket watch with the wheels and cogs turning to show the passing of time.

But however you decide to design the set each individual location can be presented very simply by moving suitcases, trunks, etc. to suggest train carriages, boats, piers, etc. The show was written so that it could be staged as economically as possible. It is important that you move between scenes quickly so as not to lose the momentum of the piece through long scene changes. Where scene changes are indicated do not black-out the lights but switch to a darker lighting state so that the audience can watch the company scurrying around creating the next setting. Sometimes the characters from the new scene can begin their dialogue whilst the characters from the previous scene are moving off. For instance, the lines announcing the passing of time can be given whilst the stage is being reset.

Use lots of background sound effects to create the locations. For example, the soft tinkle of Indian music in the Indian scenes, Chinese music in China and so on.

The costumes should be naturalistic and period 1873.

This show was originally performed by a multi-racial cast.

Phil Willmott

"As you're trudging through the day
Living life in shades of grey
Just close your eyes
Imagine that you're there!"

To my Parents
with love

ACT I

SCENE 1

1873

There is a podium set C. There are stacks of trunks, suitcases, umbrellas and junk piled high. The colours are predominately warm and sepia. During the play, props, puppets, bits of scenery and actors will emerge from the luggage. All the scenery and props will be brightly coloured by contrast. There is a higher level at the back of the stage with a doorway underneath

*A bright and breezy Overture begins (**No.1**)*

During the Overture, the Company, including Captain Fix and the Mayor, enters greeting each other

A banner unfurls which reads "The adventure starts here"

On the final notes of the Overture, there is a crack of thunder and everyone puts up an umbrella. The Company, miserable in the rain, sing on an "ah"

No 1. Eighty Days

Voice 1 (*singing*) Ev'rybody dreams of a little adventure
Voice 2   To feel the sun on your back and the wind in your hair
Voice 3   As you're trudging through the day
Voice 4   Living life in shades of grey
All   Just close your eyes, imagine you are there
   (*Loudly*)   Anywhere!

The Company put their umbrellas down

   (*Speeding up*)   Where love and adventure
               Wait at the corner
               By a magic lagoon in a tropical haze
               There are mountains and a beach
               Mighty oceans in your reach
               Can you get there but be home in eighty days?

Voice 5	Wouldn't it be perfect
	Just to pack and leave today?
Voice 6	But only if I knew I could
	Be home for Christmas Day.
Voice 7	I couldn't leave my job though
Voice 8	And I'd miss my little cat
All	But eighty days adventuring?
	I really fancy that!

Everybody dreams of a little adventure
To feel the sun on your back and the wind in your hair
As you're trudging through the day
Living life in shades of grey
Just close your eyes, imagine that you're there.

The music continues to underscore

Phileas Fogg arrives with Passepartout at his side. Fogg is handsome but imposing. Passepartout looks friendly, fun and eager to please. He speaks with a French accent

They stand with the Mayor on the podium. Everybody waves little Union Jack flags

The Mayor Welcome to Greenwich, Mr Fogg. And may I say how honoured we all are that you're starting out on your extraordinary adventure from here.

Journalist 1 Mr Fogg, I'm from the *Herald*, there's so many rumours around. Can you confirm that you've bet your entire fortune that you can travel around the world in eighty days?

Fogg It's absolutely true.

Journalist 2 But why would you risk everything?

Fogg Because when an English gentleman is serious about a wager, then he is very serious indeed. This is 1873; now that the Pan-American railway has opened up I can see no reason at all why I shouldn't be back here amongst you at twenty-one-hundred hours — nine o'clock on Christmas Day. Having of course circumnavigated the world in a mere eighty days in honour of Her Majesty Queen Victoria.

The Crowd God bless her!

Fogg Why, if man ever conquers the air he'll be able to do it even quicker.

Captain Fix emerges from the crowd. He is a swaggering but rather greasy aristocrat

Fix Poppycock! Stuff and nonsense! I know every God-forsaken corner of this wretched little planet and I tell you, it's impossible. You'll need to take trains, steamships, sail boats; even elephants — the timetables across several continents would need to match up exactly in order for you to succeed.

Fogg All taken into account, sir, it's simply a question of careful planning, calculation and trust in Bradshaw's indispensable volume of international timetables. Everything has been planned down to the finest detail.

Passepartout It's true. I've watched my master work everything out. Eighty days? Pah! If he wanted to, he could do it in two weeks!

The crowd laughs at his enthusiasm

Fogg (*drily*) Thank you, Passepartout. My valet exaggerates of course, but you see how confident we are. However, you have touched on the one thing that worries me.

Voice in Crowd What's that, Mr Fogg?

Fogg I am absolutely terrified of elephants.

Everyone laughs

Nevertheless, this evening will find us in Paris. This first scheduled stop on our historic journey.

Fix slopes back into the crowd

Crowd (*singing*) What a man, what a god
What a modern day hero
What a dream to have had
What a challenge to face
(*Softly*) And if I wasn't busy here
Then of course I'd volunteer
(*Loudly*) Hoorah for Fogg, for going in my place.

A spotlight comes up on Passepartout. Everyone else goes into slow motion

Passepartout I'm Monsieur Fogg's new servant
I started yesterday.
He promised me adventure
Et voilà! We're on our way!
I'll make the job work out,
Won't mess up like I used to do
Whereever fate may take us
He can count on Passepartout.

The scene comes back to life. The spotlight fades on Passepartout

All   Ev'rybody dreams of a little adventure
                   To feel the sun on your back and the wind in your hair
                   As you're trudging through the day
                   Living life in shades of grey
                   Just close your eyes, imagine that you're there.
                   Anywhere!
                   Where love and excitement
                   Wait at the corner
                   By a magic lagoon in a tropical haze
                   There are mountains and a beach
                   Mighty oceans in your reach
                   Can you get there but ——

Big finish

                   Be home in eighty days?

Black-out

SCENE 2

A spotlight comes up on Fix

Fix Telegram to Barings Bank, London from Captain James Fix. Instruct
     you wager all my remaining funds on Phileas Fogg failing to complete his
     round the world challenge. Stop. I shall be attending to the matter
     personally. (*He laughs nastily*)

Black-out

A spotlight comes up on a suitcase. The suitcase opens to reveal a model can-can dancer. This indicates that action has now moved to Paris

SCENE 3

The spotlight swings from the can-can dancer to light a Parisian Master of Ceremonies

MC *Mesdames et Messieurs,* ladies and gentlemen, welcome to the Moulin
     Rose, Paris's premier night-club for the lonely businessman. Without

further ado please welcome on to the stage our troupe of international beauties led by that chanteuse of the Champs-Elysées —Mademoiselle Katy O'Flathery.

The MC exits

Katy and Girls clatter into position in the darkness. Katy is wearing a preposterous Irish National Costume

The Lights come up on Katy and the Girls

No. 2. Around the World With Katy's Girls

Katy (*singing*) When I was young in Donegal
I dreamed of Paris, France
Where there were men who, I had heard,
Enjoyed artistic dance. (*Bump*)
I packed a small shillelagh
And I hailed a passing ship
Aboard were girls from ev'rywhere
All making that same trip.

Soon my friends from ev'ry nation
Joined my Paris dance sensation
"Round the World with Katy's Girls".
Marcel Proust to Gustav Eiffel
All drop in to get an eyeful
Round the world with Katy's girls

A vamp begins

So who will be your girl tonight?
Let's help you to decide

The Girls line up and introduce themselves

Svetlana Svetlana, I'm from Moscow
Won't you try my troika ride?
Helga I'm Helga from Bavaria
I'll be your special *frau.*
Yuki I'm Yuki, "want some eastern fun"?
Well, I can show you how!

Pam   I'm Pam from Alabama,
                 Won't you sit me on your knee?
Sheila   I'm Sheila from Australia,
                 The Penal Colony!

Music goes back to vamp

Trudy   I'm Trudy from the tropics
                 And I'll keep you sizzling!
Morag   I'm Morag, I'm from Scotland
                 Would you like a Highland fling?
All   Make a first-class reservation
                 To your favourite destination
                 Round the world with Katy's girls
                 Pack a toothbrush and pyjamas
                 Reykjavik to the Bahamas
                 Round the world with Katy's girls

                 Round the world with Katy's
                 Round the world with Katy's
                 Round the world with Katy's girls

Black-out

SCENE 4

The Lights come up immediately

Members of the Company re-arrange props to represent the Girls' dressing-room

Katy and her Girls are re-applying their make-up and massaging their tired feet, etc.

Sveltana It's dead out there tonight. A couple of scruffy artists, a few sailors and four drunken farmers up from the country.

The Master of Ceremonies bursts in

MC Come on, girls. I don't pay you to sit around gossiping. I want you out on that dance floor. I've got some lonely customers out there who want some female company with their flat champagne.

He exits

Sheila Chin up, girls, you never know who might walk in.

Helga That's true but you can take a pretty good guess.

Pam I wish I could meet someone nice like you did, Katy.

Trudy Yeah, but she sent him packing, didn't she?! Wasn't good enough for her.

Katy (*trying to convince herself*) I want someone better than some scruffy Charlie that can't hold down a job from one week to the next.

Helga But he was funny though ...

Pam And romantic ...

Yuki And kind of cute ...

Katy And he left Paris six months ago tonight, promising to make our fortune and I haven't heard a word from him since.

Passepartout bursts in

Passepartout Hallo, girls!

Girls Passepartout!

The Girls mob Passepartout. Katy remains distant

Passepartout (*to Katy*) And how's my favourite girl?

Katy (*spikey*) I'm very well. Thank you very much for asking. Why didn't you write to me?

Passepartout I didn't want to write until I had some good news to tell you.

Katy And ...

Passepartout Oh, baby, you're looking at a made man. (*He sings*)

No. 3 Passepartout

This time it's gonna be so diff'rent from before
Goodbye to scraping by
So long to being poor.
In eighty days you're going to see
There's no reason
Why you shouldn't be my baby.
I know I haven't been much of a catch before
I know you said you wanted more
But I'm changing
Rearranging
Look who's coming through
Passepartout
Passepartout
Passepartout!

Katy   I've heard it all before
                      I'm sick of your schemes
                      I'm tired of being broke
                      And living on dreams
                      I want more, I can't carry on like this
                      Don't think you can win me round
                      With your codswallop.

Passepartout   Maybe you've heard of an intrepid Englishman
                      Racing around the world,
                      At least that is the plan.
                      See, he's got to get home by Christmas Day
                      Or he loses ev'rything
                      That he has wagered.
                      He's planned it brilliantly, the route, the time, the speed.
                      England has bet he will succeed.
                      You're observant
                      Who's his servant?
                      I'll give you a clue
                      Passepartout
                      Passepartout
                      Passepartout!

                      It's going to make me famous
                      I'll make you proud.
                      We'll take a carriage ride
                      And wave at the crowd.
                      They'll start cheering when I propose to you
                      What's that face for? Baby,
                      I'm not fibbing this time.

The Girls try to lighten Katy's mood by catching her up in a dance. Eventually she can't hold out any longer and she joins in, delighted to be reunited with Passepartout

   The Waiters and kitchen staff of the Moulin Rose tumble in. They carry trays and saucepans. They are happy to see Passepartout

Passepartout greets them excitedly

There is a hub-bub of conversation — "Passepartout! Welcome back! Where have you been? Good to see you my friend!" etc.

Dance break. Passepartout and Katy lead everyone in a parade. They are carried shoulder high. Everyone else bangs and clatters trays and saucepans, etc. in time to the music

All	This time it's gonna be so different to before
	Goodbye to scraping by
	So long to being poor
	In eighty days you're going to see
	There's no reason
	Why he shouldn't be your baby
	I know he hasn't been much of a catch before
	I know you said you wanted more.
Girls	So he's changing
	Rearranging
	Look who's coming through
Passepartout	Passepartout
	Passepartout
	Passepartout!
Men	Phileas Fogg's
	Devoted slave
	His servant, friend and crew
All	Passepartout
	Passepartout
	Passepartout!
Passepartout	Coming through
	Coming through
	Coming through
All (*half time*)	Passepartout
	Passepartout
	Passepar ——

Passepartout (*speaking*) *Zut alors!* I have to find Monsieur Fogg a copy of the London *Times* by precisely 08.34 or I'm out of a job.

Passepartout rushes out then immediately rushes back in. He pecks Katy on the cheek

(*Singing*)   I love you!

Black-out

SCENE 5

There is the sound of a railway station in Paris

The Lights come up on Captain Fix. He rubs his hands together with pleasure before laughing nastily and disappearing into the crowd

Members of the Company cross the stage as passengers, carrying luggage

One of the Company announces to the audience, " October, ninth. Seventy-seven days to go"

Fogg enters. He is followed by Passepartout arguing with a Parisian Railway Porter. Passepartout carries a carpet bag

Passepartout This is absolutely ridiculous. I did not cancel my master's reservation for this train.
Porter Well somebody did, monsieur. And now there are no seats left.
Passepartout But you don't understand, it's very important that we are on that train.
Porter I'm sorry, sir, but the train is full and as you cancelled your reservation …
Passepartout But I'm telling you I did no such thing!

The Porter shrugs and waves his flag

  Fix crosses the stage, tips his hat to Fogg and exits

Fogg doesn't notice Fix

There is the sound of the train leaving

Passepartout What are we going to do, master? We'll miss our ferry connection now!
Fogg (*completely calm*) Yes, Passepartout, I realize that. I'll take over now, thank you very much. (*To the Porter*) My dear fellow, you seem an ingenious sort of chap. Tell me, if you were a man of some means and you needed to beat that train to its destination, what would you do?
Porter It is quite impossible, monsieur. There is not another train until midday tomorrow.
Fogg But, if you were a man of some *considerable* means …
Passepartout (*clutching the carpet bag*) We've got a big bag of money!
Fogg Yes, thank you, Passepartout.
Porter You could have all the money in the world but the only way to beat the train would be if you could go directly over the Alps rather than following the snaking railway track it's … Just a minute, did you say considerable means?

Fogg I did.

Porter Then, I think I should take you to meet the love of my life.

Passepartout You buffoon! Mr Fogg has no time to meet pretty girls.

Porter Perhaps you'd like to see a picture of her. (*He holds out a picture*)

Passepartout and Fogg look at the picture and exchange glances

Passepartout I see what you mean. What a beauty.

Porter She's yours for the right price.

Fogg What *is* the going rate for a hot air balloon? I'll double it.

The Lights change

SCENE 6

The exchange between Disraeli and Queen Victoria is tightly lit

During the following, in the surrounding darkness, an open laundry or costume basket with sandbags attached is set and Fogg and Passepartout climb into it. Members of the Company take their positions for SCENE 7

There is a blast of music (**No.4**)

Disraeli enters

Voice (*off*) Her Majesty Queen Victoria.

Queen Victoria enters

Queen Victoria Prime Minister Disraeli.

Disraeli I came as soon as I could, Marm.

Queen Victoria I hear there've been extraordinary developments. A fever of gambling is sweeping the Empire.

Disraeli It would seem so, Marm.

Queen Victoria Phileas Fogg is attempting to cross Europe in a hot air balloon.

Disraeli So I believe, your Majesty.

Queen Victoria I cannot condone gambling, Mr Disraeli.

Disraeli Of course not, your Majesty.

Queen Victoria But, Mr Disraeli.

Disraeli Yes, your Majesty?

Queen Victoria Here's one hundred guineas. Please wager it on Mr Fogg succeeding.

The lighting begins to change

They exit

SCENE 7

The following sequence should run without any breaks for scenery changes, etc. The different locations should be suggested with lights and physical action, perhaps as described below

The Company stand around the basket holding birds on sticks and open umbrellas painted with clouds

As the Lights come up fully, one of the birds perches on the edge of the basket

Passepartout (*to the bird*) Shoo! Shoo!

The bird "flies" off

Master, I cannot find the instruction booklet that our friend said would be in the basket.

Fogg It's perfectly simple, Passepartout; if you wish the balloon to go higher you drop one of the sandbags like so. (*He drops one of the sandbags*)

The actors lower the umbrella clouds giving the impression that the balloon is rising

If you wish to move forward you simply pull on the gas like this. (*He reaches up and mimes pulling a lever*)

There is the sound of a blast of gas. The clouds all move accordingly as if the balloon is moving through them

Passepartout This is fun! Where are we now, boss?

Fogg According to my calculations, when the cloud clears we should be able to land in Switzerland.

The umbrella clouds cover Fogg and Passepartout so that the balloon can be unobserved

During the following, unseen, some very Spanish Dancers enter and join Fogg and Passepartout in the basket

Sherlock Holmes and Watson enter. Sherlock Holmes reads a newspaper

Holmes Good heavens, Watson!

Watson What is it, Holmes? Another outrage in the baffling case of *The Hound of the Baskervilles*?

Holmes I'm afraid it's worse than that, old friend. Fogg should be over the Alps by now.

Watson Has there been a hiccup?

Holmes I'm afraid so.

Watson Well, conditions are very cloudy. I expect their co-ordinates are out a couple of degrees.

Holmes I'm afraid the geographical error was a little more elementary, my dear Watson.

The umbrella clouds move to one side to reveal Fogg, Passepartout and the Spanish Dancers

Dancer Welcome to Madrid, Señor Fogg.

Passepartout (*stamping*) *¡Olé!*

Fogg glares at him

Black-out

Immediately the Lights come up on a model balloon high above the set. The umbrella clouds move to obscure the basket once more

When the basket is obscured, the Dancers exit and a Gondolier enters the balloon unseen

Fogg (*voice only*) There's a fair wind today. We should be well on course to make Tunisia by suppertime.

The Lights fade on the balloon and return to the previous state. The clouds part to reveal Fogg and Passepartout talking to a Gondolier

Gondolier (*singing*) Welcome to Venice
                         In Italy.
(*Speaking*) *Buon Giorno*, Mister Fogg! You want some nice ravioli for your supper?

The umbrella clouds move to obscure the basket. Unobserved, Fogg and Passepartout climb out of the basket and the basket is cleared away

The Gondolier exits with the basket

The Lights darken

There are jungle noises

Livingstone, a ragged English explorer, and Stanley enter. They greet one another

Stanley Doctor Livingstone, I presume.
Livingstone At last you've found me, Stanley. How extraordinary to see someone outside of the tribe. I've been cut off from the rest of the world for an age now. Give me some news from dear old England, I beg of you.
Stanley They say Phileas Fogg aims to land in Libya today.
Livingstone God bless him.

They exit

The umbrella clouds move apart to reveal Fogg and Passepartout

Some Greek Dancers enter

Fogg and Passepartout watch as they pass by

A Tour Guide enters

Tour Guide Welcome to Athens. You want for me to give you a tour of the Acropolis?

The Lights change

Passepartout, Fogg, the Greek Dancers and Tour Guide rush off. The Company with the clouds also exit

The sand dance music

Katy appears in a spotlight reading a postcard

Egyptian sand dancers enter behind Katy and pass by

Katy (*reading*) "*Ma chère* Katy. At last we have arrived in Suez, Egypt and have had a stroke of extraordinary luck. The captain of a powerful new steam ship has guaranteed to help us arrive in India on schedule. This time next week we shall be in Bombay!"

She exits

There is a cymbal crash and a shaft of light hits a suitcase. It opens to reveal a beautiful little pop-up Taj Mahal

A few props are quickly rearranged to represent the hotel lobby

Fogg and Passepartout enter and wait c. *At the same time an Announcer enters*

Announcer Thirteenth, October. Seventy-three days to go!

The Lights change

The Announcer exits

SCENE 8

A hotel Concierge, magnificently dressed in white and gold and wearing a turban, enters and bows

Concierge Welcome to the Bombay Hilton, esteemed European guests. We had heard that you may be a day or so later than you planned.

Fogg Certainly not. What an extraordinary idea! Everything should be according to our reservation. You have set aside your London suite I believe. I hear it has been decorated to resemble the Reform Club in Pall Mall. After weeks of staying in the most regrettable circumstances, that will be most acceptable.

Concierge I'm afraid there has been a change to your room allocation, Mr Fogg. You see we had heard you were detained for a few days, the suite of rooms is one of our largest and we received an urgent request from an Indian royal family. As you'll understand, a royal visit requires sufficient space to also accommodate a significant entourage so we took the liberty of offering the party the London suite. Happily, however, we are able to accommodate you in our beautiful Maharaja rooms. Although somewhat smaller the suite is lavishly appointed in the style of an Indian palace. I trust you will find it a more than adequate substitute.

Fogg pointedly takes off his top hat and passes it to Passepartout. He knows this means trouble

Passepartout Uh-oh!

Fogg I'm afraid I have no desire to be surrounded by the trappings of an Indian palace. My servant will tell you that I am not a great enthusiast of foreign travel. I do not indulge in sightseeing, I do not sample local delicacies, and I do not enjoy displays of colourful local customs. I don't doubt that others find them most diverting. I, however, prefer to seek an environment as close as possible to that which I enjoy at home, where I may play at whist and partake of the menu I have enjoyed for the past thirty-five years. Tonight, being Thursday, I look forward to my usual Thursday dinner of boiled fish with Reading sauce, roast beef garnished with mushrooms, rhubarb and gooseberry tart ——

Passepartout —— and a slice of Cheshire cheese.

Fogg All of which I trust you will be able to provide.

Concierge With some difficulty, sir, but I believe so.
Fogg Excellent. And your London suite sounds exactly the environment in which to enjoy it. I am not an unreasonable man. I shall be studying my Bradshaw's universal timetable here in your lobby for the next half an hour, which will, I trust, be sufficient time for you to clear my room. Please give its current occupants my sincerest regards and I trust they will enjoy the local splendour of your Maharaja suite. Should any member of the party wish to discuss the matter further they will find me over there. That will be all. Thank you. (*He turns and settles down with a book*)

The Concierge bows, sighs to himself, and moves off

Passepartout attempts to sneak out behind Fogg's back as he reads

Fogg Passepartout.
Passepartout Yes, sir!
Fogg Where are you going?

In the background, the young and beautiful Princess Aouda enters with the Concierge. The Concierge points to Fogg and the Princess smiles in response. The Concierge bows and moves off. The Princess observes the following exchange

Passepartout Well, I thought I'd see a little bit of the city. I hear it's a very beautiful and fascinating place
Fogg I'm sure it's no more beautiful than St James's Park when the blossom is out or any more fascinating than the Reading Room of the British Museum. I strictly forbid you to leave the hotel. So far we have been lucky and we are not a day ahead or behind schedule. However, it is absolutely imperative that we catch our train to Calcutta or our plans are thwarted. I cannot risk you getting lost in a strange and inhospitable city.
Aouda I think your friend will find our country most hospitable if he is able to treat my countrymen with the same politeness and respect that they will offer him. Good-afternoon. Mr Fogg, I presume? I am Princess Aouda.
Fogg Good-afternoon, your Majesty, and may I compliment you on your miraculous command of the English language.
Aouda Hardly miraculous, Mr Fogg. My mother was English and my father sent me to be educated in England from an early age.
Fogg I understand. That is quite common all over the world. Fathers of minor foreign aristocracy naturally hope their daughters will bag a fine English husband.
Aouda On the contrary. I can think of nothing my father would have hated more. As an infant I was betrothed in marriage to a neighbouring Maharaja.

I cannot imagine why he would wish me to align myself to a boorish prig of an Englishman. My command of English has however prevented my people being fleeced by yours on several occasions. You are the gentleman who is insisting on my vacating my suite of rooms?

Fogg If it is entirely convenient.

Aouda It is not convenient at all. However, it apparently means a great deal to you and my father always taught me to take advantage of any opportunity to help others. Something my time amongst the narrow-minded English did not alter. (*To Passepartout*) Sir, if you are interested in seeing our beautiful city I'm sure I can spare you one of my servants to show you around.

Fogg Thank you, but my valet has no desire to mingle amongst small-minded savages.

Aouda Then I trust he will assiduously avoid the English upper-class.

The Concierge returns

Concierge Mr Fogg, in light of the unfortunate mix-up with the rooms I have taken the liberty of preparing a table in our restaurant where you can enjoy your delicious boiled fish and rhubarb.

Fogg Is it secluded?

Concierge Oh quite, sir.

Fogg Good. I would hate to be disturbed any further by the squawking of female natives.

Fogg strides out, followed by the Concierge

Passepartout On behalf of my master may I thank you very much for allowing us to change rooms.

Aouda Not at all.

Passepartout I know he seems a little odd but he is under an awful lot of pressure.

Aouda No need to explain. Englishmen like Mr Fogg can always find an excuse for badly treating others.

Passepartout He is not so bad. We must remember to ... What is their expression? "Keep our chin up"!

Aouda That's exactly what my English mother used to say when I was a young princess.

Passepartout It's still good advice.

Aouda I wish things seemed as straightforward as they did then. Enjoy your stay in India, monsieur.

Passepartout begins to move towards the exit

Passepartout Thank you, your Highness.

He exits

Alone, the Princess becomes vulnerable. She sings

No. 5 The Maharaja's Child

Aouda   Back when I was young it wasn't hard to be a princess
For guidance I could ask the king and queen
When rebels stormed our palace then
My parents both were killed
And every day I'm haunted by the scene.
Well this is now
It isn't then
They banished me to England. I was ten.
They stole my throne, the Maharaja's child
It feels so strange to be back here again.

Someone, somewhere help me
Don't leave me here alone
Tearing up the rule book
Like my mother tried.
Trapped between two worlds
Within a modern day and age
I don't mind admitting that I'm terrified.

In stories I remember it was nice to be a princess
In fairy tales you got to choose a prince
In real life there's only frogs
You face your foes alone
With many fearsome dragons to convince.
Well this is now
It isn't then
Tradition says I marry as I'm told
My country's weak we need alliances
So I belong to one who's cruel and old.

If only he were young
If only he were kind
If only my new husband knew the world I leave behind
We could form a modern state
Our people could unite
But he's just a brutal ancient tyrant spoiling for a fight.

> Someone, somewhere help me
> Don't leave me here alone
> Tearing up the rule book
> Like my mother tried.
> Trapped between two worlds
> Within a modern day and age
> I don't mind admitting that I'm terrified.

Black-out

She exits

SCENE 9

The Lights come up on Passepartout, bored, in the hotel lobby. Fix is hidden behind a newspaper

Passepartout So, five hours until we catch our train and I'm not to leave the hotel. Whatever shall I do? I wonder if anyone wants a game of Boules.

Fix is still hidden

Fix Excuse me.

Passepartout Monsieur!

Fix (*emerging*) Are you, by any chance, the legendary Parisian gentleman who's accompanying Phileas Fogg in his attempt to circumnavigate the world in eighty days?

Passepartout That's right, monsieur. How did you know?

Fix The newspapers in Paris speak of nothing else: your bravery; your intelligence; your stamina. There was even a rather handsome lithograph of you wrestling a wild boar to the ground.

Passepartout My picture was in the paper?

Fix Everyone has placed a wager, including myself.

Passepartout Your money is safe, monsieur. Mr Fogg and I will win our challenge for you.

Fix Well, I'm afraid I've put rather a large sum of money on you failing. You see, I just can't believe that anyone could be as fearless as the papers say that you are.

Passepartout (*affronted*) But, monsieur ——

Fix Besides, the world is a dangerous place; all sorts of unexpected perils await even the most seasoned traveller.

Passepartout Oh, not my master, he has planned for every eventuality.

Fix Well we shall see, monsieur, we shall see! But should you not be rushing for a train?

Passepartout It does not leave until this evening.

Fix How fortuitous. Allow me to introduce myself. Captain James Fix, the famous big game hunter. Perhaps you've heard of me? If you're free this afternoon I should be honoured if you'd accompany me on a little shooting expedition.

Passepartout Well, you see I would but my master he is most insistent I don't leave the hotel. It is very important that we catch our train to Calcutta.

Fix Please, please. You don't have to explain. I was right, the newspapers obviously overestimated your bravery or perhaps they mistook you for someone else.

Passepartout I am no coward, monsieur.

Fix After all the French are not renowned for their pluck.

Passepartout How dare you, monsieur! I have been known to be very plucky.

Fix What a shame then that you must spend your afternoon nurse-maiding your master when you could be out with me, enjoying the thrill of a big game hunt. Have you never hunted, monsieur?

Passepartout No, I haven't. Perhaps Mr Fogg will not miss me. I know it is his custom to now retire for an afternoon of study and cards and he does not like me to disturb him.

Fix Then what are we waiting for?

Passepartout But I don't know ...

Fix makes towards the exit

Fix Good-day, sir.

Passepartout Is it fun shooting things?

Fix Oh, my dear boy, let me tell you. (*He picks up an umbrella, which he will use as a rifle and sings*)

No. 6 Bang!

When I was small it gave me a thrill
If ever I had a chance I would kill.
Pulling the wings off butterflies was my hobby.
How could they blame me, was it my fault
When Nanny bought my first catapult?
Naturally I would terrify cats and doggies.
There's a thrill in mindless cruelty
Screams of pain were always fuel to me,
Using a gun's
My kind of fun
Let me tell you how it's done.

Look, there's goes a tiger cub
Bang! Now it's a lovely rug.
Gosh! There goes a jaguar,
Bang! Now, it's an *objet d'art*
Oooh! Look at the bunnykins now.
Bang! Send for their next of kins now
Bang! How it makes me shiver
Bang! Bang! Bang!

Naturally giv'n the talent I had
The army was perfect for this growing lad
Seeing the world then getting the chance for shootin'
Wasn't so good with discipline though
Marching was boring, wanted to go
Into the fray and viciously put the boot in.
Single-handed wiped out the enemy
Plus the man who tried to teach drill to me.
Soon, though, I wore
Medals galore
Let me tell you what they're for.

Bang! Got someone in your sights?
Bang! Why not put out their lights
Bang! You've evened up the score
Bang! They won't come back for more
Bang! I get quite demented,
Bang! Making the late lamented
Bang! How it makes me shiver.
Bang! Bang! Bang!

The Lights change

Fix and Passepartout hide as if they are in tall grass. They are hoping to shoot something. As an option, the umbrella can be swapped for a rifle

Right, here's an excellent game hunting spot,
Natural beauty awaiting your shot.
Time for us men to step in and make a killing.
There in the bushes I saw something move.
Don't be afraid, take my rifle and prove
You can be cold-hearted, ruthlessly able and willing.
Aim with care, there is no second chance
Fill its head with lead and watch it dance.

> Make me a fan
> That's if you can
> Prove yourself a real man.
>
> Bang! Hallo there young gorilla
> Oops I pulled the trigger,
> Bang! I could never stand a ——
> Bang! Live and kicking panda.
> Bang! That's the way to treat these ——
> Bang! alleged endangered species
> Quick before it scarpers.
> Bang!

Passepartout   I ——
Fix   Bang!
Passepartout   But ——
Fix   Bang! Bang!

Passepartout fires. There is the sound of a sharp gun shot, followed by a distressed mooing

> Oh, dear. I'm afraid you've shot one of the temple's sacred cows. Quite absurd the ridiculous fuss these people make about those creatures. I do so hope you can still catch your train. Oh well, must be going. It's been fun, hasn't it?

Fix starts to move off. Passepartout is left looking shell-shocked

Fix (*singing*)   Bang! How it makes me shiver!
                              Bang! Bang! Bang!
                              Gotcha!

Black-out

There is the sound of a train pulling out, an angry crowd and cows mooing, etc.

Announcer October, twenty-seventh. Fifty-nine days left!

SCENE 10

When the Lights come up, Fogg is sitting calmly playing patience in a train carriage. An anxious Passepartout sits opposite

There is the sound of a train running

Passepartout But please, master, let me explain what happened.

Fogg No explanation is necessary. You made the train with three seconds to spare. It is perhaps regrettable that your clothes were ripped, your nose was bloodied and you were pursued by a large stone-wielding mob.

Passepartout But they had every right to be upset.

Fogg I don't doubt it.

Passepartout If I could just explain, it wasn't my fault.

Fogg I have no idea. But I feel certain that your behaviour is incompatible with the calm decorum with which I wish to conduct this expedition. Which is why I am considering dispensing with your services.

Passepartout Mr Fogg, please don't fire me. What will I tell my girl?

Fogg I will of course provide you with sufficient funds with which to return to Europe.

Passepartout But, I don't want to go back. I like seeing all the different countries — even though we're moving so fast that they're all a bit blurry.

Fogg It is the nature of our mission here that we travel with pinpoint accuracy from place to place. Unfortunately there is no time to spare for sightseeing or instigating riots at railway stations. Do I make myself clear?

Passepartout Perfectly clear, master. Everything will go exactly to plan now. Passepartout will make sure of it.

There is the sound of brakes screeching and the train coming to a halt

Fogg looks at his watch

Fogg Odd, an unscheduled stop. This is a British East India Company train.

Passepartout Don't worry about a thing, master. I'll sort it out.

Fogg I shall be in the restaurant car taking my accustomed afternoon tea.

Passepartout Of course, monsieur.

Fogg leaves. A British Guard enters

Guard All change. Everybody off.

Passepartout What do you mean, "everybody off"? We're in the middle of the Indian jungle.

Guard That's right, sir, and this is where we run out of track.

Passepartout But this is the train to Calcutta.

Guard Well, it's the Calcutta line. Trouble is, it's not finished yet. This is as far as the track goes at the moment. We hope to have the whole thing finished by the next monsoon season though.

Passepartout But how are we to get to Calcutta?

Guard I'm afraid you can't, sir. Well, unless you can find some way of getting through the jungle to Allahabad and picking up another train there. I wouldn't recommend you leave this village, sir. This is Nizam territory, very dangerous.

Black-out

Music underscoring (**No.6b**)

SCENE 11

As the Lights come up, Queen Victoria and Disraeli enter. She is looking at a globe and he is sipping tea

During the following, the setting is rearranged for the following scene

Queen Victoria Where has Mr Fogg reached this morning, Prime Minister?
Disraeli No-one knows, your Majesty. He is lost in the Indian jungle on his way to Calcutta.
Queen Victoria A most inhospitable terrain as I recall.
Disraeli Quite so, Marm. Our experts predict he will be endeavouring to reach Allahabad.
Queen Victoria Just a moment, isn't that the Nizam region?
Disraeli I fear so, your Majesty.
Queen Victoria And that bloodthirsty tyrant Ferrighea has just passed away. Isn't it Nizam custom to burn the queen alive along with the body of her dead husband?
Disraeli Indeed, your Majesty.
Queen Victoria His poor wife, the thought of ... (*She shudders*) A barbaric people. Do you think Mr Fogg realizes the danger he's in?
Disraeli We very much doubt Mr Fogg has been able to penetrate far into the jungle on foot. The going is very slow for even the most experienced trackers and there is no other form of transport.
Queen Victoria Oh dear, it would seem his expedition and my hundred-guinea wager may be doomed.

Black-out

Music underscoring (**No. 6c**)

   They exit

SCENE 12

The Lights come up on Passepartout and Fogg riding on an elephant's back. This was originally performed by Fogg and Passepartout seated high on a platform behind a life-sized puppet elephant head. Fogg looks very alarmed

Passepartout Nice and smoothly, Monsieur Elephant, if you please. Mr Fogg is frightened.

Fogg I certainly am not frightened. It just never entered my calculations that I should have to meet one of these infernal creatures, let alone ride on the back of one.

Passepartout But I did well to find him, master.

Fogg You have my eternal gratitude, Passepartout. Certainly no amount of cash would induce those farmers to lend us their beasts and journey beyond the village during the funeral of King Ferrighea.

Passepartout I don't like the sound of him.

Fogg You're quite right. It would be better if we could move a little faster before nightfall.

Passepartout I don't think that Eugene is very happy.

Fogg Eugene?

Passepartout Our elephant.

Fogg Why is he called Eugene?

Passepartout The farmer who sold him to me says he is no good for helping to make baby elephants. He does not like the ladies. Like my friend Eugene who works at the opera house.

Fogg That is quite ridiculous. Is that what makes him unhappy?

Passepartout He thinks you do not like him, Mr Fogg. That is why he walks slowly. He is sad. I have even given him the little French flag so he can feel proud. But he shows no enthusiasm for waving it at the baboons.

Fogg Please tell him I think he is a very splendid elephant.

Passepartout Did you hear that Eugene? It is no good he does not believe you. Why don't you sing him a little song?

Fogg I do not sing little songs. I am certainly not singing to an elephant.

Passepartout Poor Eugene. He is so sad. And the sun is setting. If only he was happy and he could carry us out of danger. Just a little song, master.

Fogg What could I possibly sing to him? I don't know any elephant songs.

Passepartout There's a good jungle song they sing at the music hall. It is very romantic. Simple to learn, you could pick it up very quickly.

Fogg Well, perhaps you'd better teach it to me. But I warn you if anyone ever hears about this back in London …

Passepartout Eugene, me and Mr Fogg, the famous adventurer, are going to sing you a little song. (*He sings*)

No. 7 Jungle Honeymoon

Famous brave adventurer Caractacus Fife
Felt a little lonely so he took him a wife
He kissed her very sweetly then he gave her a smile
And told her to start packing for a trip up the Nile.

           Elephants went
           Trump, trump, trump,
           Trump, trumpity, trump!
           Baboons went
           Boo, boo, boo
           Boo, boopity, boo!
           Chimpanzees went cha, cha, cha!
           Happy hippos ha, ha, ha
           On the honky-tonky jungle honeymoon.

The music continues to underscore

Fogg I am not singing that!
Passepartout Master, don't be afraid. I'll count you in.

Fogg very reluctantly speaks his bits to the music

	Elephants went
Fogg	Trump, trump, trump,
	Trump, trumpity, trump!
Passepartout	Baboons went
Fogg	Boo, boo, boo,
	Boo, boopity, boo!
Passepartout	Chimpanzees went
Fogg	Cha, cha, cha!
Passepartout	Happy hippos
Fogg	Ha, ha, ha!
	On the honky-tonky jungle honeymoon.

The elephant pricks up its ears, raises its eyebrows and trumpets

Passepartout (*speaking*) He likes it. Quickly, we'd better sing it again.

They sing the song again. As the tune gets faster they bounce up and down faster, so it looks as if the elephant has speeded up

Fogg   ⎫   Elephants went
Passepartout ⎬   Trump, trump, trump,
                  Trump, trumpity, trump!
                  Baboons went
                  Boo, boo, boo
                  Boo, boopity, boo!
                  Chimpanzees went cha, cha, cha!
                  Happy hippos ha, ha, ha!
                  On the honky-tonky jungle honeymoon.

The lighting grows darker

SCENE 13

The lighting is dark and oppressive. There are threatening jungle noises

Passepartout I think Eugene needs a rest now.
Fogg I'm afraid that's not advisable, not yet. We're still deep in Nizam territory.

A funeral chant begins off stage (**No. 8 The Nizam**)

Passepartout What's that?
Fogg It sounds ominous.
Passepartout Get down, Eugene!

The elephant's head appears to duck out of sight

> *During the following, many Priests enter and fill the stage chanting and funeral dancing. They are dressed in red and wear fierce animal masks. They carry on a body and place it into a trunk or trapdoor in the floor*

The trapdoor or trunk is full of smoke and red light

Fogg and Passepartout watch unobserved

Fogg I'm afraid it couldn't be worse. We seem to have stumbled upon the very funeral of King Ferrighea himself. That must be his body they've brought here for the ritual burning.
Passepartout Burning!
Fogg That's not all. You see their obscure and fundamentalist traditions also dictate that his bride is burnt alive alongside him. The rest of India is as appalled as we are by this barbarism.

> *Princess Aouda, doped, is dragged in by the Priests*

Passepartout Master! Master! Look it's Princess Aouda from the hotel. But surely they cannot mean to ...?
Fogg Great heavens it looks as if they're preparing her for the fire.
Passepartout But this is horrible. We have to do something. What's the matter with her? She looks as if she's sleepwalking.
Fogg They'll have drugged her with hemp fumes to stop her escaping.
Passepartout What can we do? There's only two of us, well, three with Eugene.

Fogg Well, whatever it is we're going to have to do it quickly. I'll go and have a scout around. You stay out of sight and try and avoid attracting a riot this time or any more singing elephants.

The Priests perform an exciting dance making terrifying animal noises. They circle around Princess Aouda; spinning her, passing her around the circle, thwarting her attempts to escape and pushing her towards the funeral fire .
During the dance, Fogg, unseen by the audience, swaps with the corpse

At the climax of the dance and just as Princess Aouda is to be thrown into the fire, the corpse of the dead Maharaja seems to rise up from the grave, covered by a shroud

The Priests rush off in terror

The shroud falls away to reveal it is Fogg. He scoops Princess Aouda up in his arms, rather dashingly in the fireglow. Passepartout rushes to join them

Passepartout Eugene! Eugene!

Black-out

Dim Lights come up for the scene change

SCENE 14

There is the sound of a train. A carriage is assembled to make the train

As the lighting comes up, Passepartout and Fogg take their places on the train. They sit opposite each other

Fogg How is Princess Aouda this morning? We arrive in Calcutta soon.
Passepartout I just took her a cup of tea. She is still very shaken but she knows she is safe. We will take her with us, won't we, master? We can't leave her in India, she's so frightened those madmen will capture her again.
Fogg We will deliver her safely to her relatives in Hong Kong.
Passepartout But that might slow us down.
Fogg It is of no matter.
Passepartout You see, I always knew you had a heart.
Fogg Heart doesn't come into it. We are on schedule and subsequently can allow a little human emotion to intrude for the half-hour it will take to track

down her family residence.

Passepartout Then all is going well for us, is it not, master? Eugene likes his new home, helping with the tea harvest. Princess Aouda is getting better and you and I are on our way to winning your wager. I think I shall write to my Katy and tell her she is going to be very proud of me.

There is the sound of the train arriving

Fogg And here we are at our next port of call. (*He looks at his watch*) All of fifteen minutes ahead of schedule. (*He looks out of the window*) My goodness me. I wonder what the commotion's all about.

A Guard enters

Guard Mr Fogg, there's a delegation to see you.

Fogg How extraordinary. Perhaps it's a party from the British Embassy with some paperwork regarding our visas to China. You may write your letter whilst I attend to the matter, then make sure the luggage is sent over for the seven o'clock sailing to Hong Kong.

Passepartout Master, it is I, Passepartout. You know I never let you down.

Fogg leaves

Passepartout writes a postcard to Katy. He sings

No. 9 Passepartout — Reprise

Baby, your honey is the star of India
Ev'ryone loves me, I'm the prince of popular.
Maharajas ask me around for tea,
I astound them with the way
I've planned our wedding.
Soon you'll be walking with me
Down that blessed aisle,
Always I'm dreaming of your smile.
No more space now
Got to race now.
All my love to you,
Passepartout,
Passepartout ——

Fogg enters

Fogg Passepartout, you will please come with me.

Passepartout What about the luggage? Shall I send it round to the boat now?

Fogg There will be no need. The luggage isn't going anywhere. We are not going anywhere. My visitor was indeed the British ambassador with a delegation from the Hindu community in Calcutta, where it seems you shot a cow sacred to their religion.

During the following, the Company gradually fill the shadows at the edge of the stage. They stare accusingly at Passepartout

The British authorities take a very dim view of disrespectful behaviour toward the native population in the interest of maintaining harmony here and I have to say I completely concur with their wisdom in this matter. You have committed one of the greatest outrages anyone can remember. The minimum penance required by custom for the harming of such an animal is that you fast and ask forgiveness at the temple for thirty days and nights. I, as your master, am required to join you. We begin our term at once. Our adventure is over. The wager is lost.

Ensemble (*singing; slowly*)
                    Look who's thrown it,
                    Look who's blown it
                    Look who's in the stew.
(*Accusatory*)   Passepartout!
                    Passepartout!
(*Pathetically*)   Passepartout.

Black-out

No. 10 Entr'acte

ACT II

SCENE 1

Holmes and Watson enter

Sherlock Holmes Why the furrowed brow, my dear, Watson?

Dr Watson I must confess I'm completely at a loss to solve this one. Inspector Lestrade tells me that Phileas Fogg may win his wager yet but the last I heard he was unavoidably detained in India. How has he got back on schedule? Great heavens, does the man have supernatural powers?

Sherlock Holmes Better than that, old fellow. He's got a large carpetbag of money. Or rather he did have. According to *The Times*, once the Indian authorities saw how contrite our fellows were, and heard about the adventure at foot they satisfied themselves with a large donation to restore an ancient temple. Fogg left on the next high tide.

Dr Watson Great heavens! He has the luck of the devil.

Sherlock Holmes Not quite, it's still going to be a struggle getting back on schedule, particularly as he's now missed a vital sea crossing to Japan with no other steamer timetabled for twelve hours. And he's now lost most of his funds.

Dr Watson So our wager isn't won yet?

Sherlock Holmes Far from it, I'm afraid.

Dr Watson And where are Fogg and his party now?

Sherlock Holmes It would seem as if they're unavoidably marooned in Hong Kong.

*There is a blast of Chinese music (**No. 11**)*

A suitcase opens to reveal a model of a Chinese Building

Announcer (*voice only*) Eleventh November! Forty-four days to go!

Holmes and Watson exit as Passepartout enters

SCENE 2

Chinese banners unfurl

A Chinese dragon weaves its way around the stage. It nuzzles up to Passepartout

Passeparout looks very miserable

No. 11 Sorry Dragon

Passepartout (*singing*)
> Life is full of ups and downs
> I've often heard that old cliché
> Well someone somewhere's
> Taken all my share of ups
> So things only go the other way.
> The French are clever, never fools
> So why is life a lot of boules?
> I've lost the wager,
> Lost the trust of Monsieur Fogg
> And lost my fiancée.
>
> Sorry, dragon,
> I can't dance with you
> Sorry, dragon,
> Just too sad and blue
> Sorry, dragon,
> I'd make you sorry too

Princess Aouda enters on the other side of the stage

The Dragon notices and goes over to her

Aouda
> A stranger in a foreign land
> A fugitive where I belong
> How can everything
> In life be crystal clear
> Then go so very wrong?
> How ever did I end up here?
> Will anything be quite the same?
> Racing round the world behind
> The pompous Fogg
> In this silly schoolboy game.
>
> Sorry, dragon,
> I can't dance with you
> Sorry, dragon,
> Just too sad and blue
> Sorry, dragon,
> I'd make you sorry too.

The music continues

Passepartout (*speaking*) Dear Monsieur Fogg, ever since you engaged me
in your service I have messed things up for you. I wanted so much for us
to make it around the world in eighty days but I have been a disaster every
step of the way and now you have had to pay all your funds to get me out
of trouble. I think you and Princess Aouda will be much better off without
me. I will not trouble you again. Yours faithfully, Jean Passepartout. PS.
You need to buy some new socks and your pearl cufflinks are in the left
hand drawer of your cabin trunk.

(*Singing*)	Never thought I'd feel so sad
Aouda	Never thought I'd leave my land
Passepartout	Never thought I'd wish
	The ground would eat me up
Aouda	Or lose each dream I'd planned
Passepartout	What a mess I'm in again
Aouda	Lost the only life I've known.
Aouda ⎤	Who would ever guess
Passeparout ⎦	It would end like this
	And I'd feel so alone.
	Sorry, dragon,
	I can't dance with you
	Sorry, dragon,
	Just too sad and blue
	Sorry, dragon,
	I'd make you sorry too.

Aouda exits

SCENE 3

Passepartout is distracted by a commotion behind him

*A circus barker, Barnum, crosses the stage with a Chinese Interpreter.
Barnum carries a playbill*

The Interpreter repeats everything he says in Chinese

A crowd gathers excitedly

Barnum Roll up! Roll up! Get your tickets here for Barnum and Bailey's Circus. Last Hong Kong shows before we leave for Japan. See the world famous Indian elephants. New this season! Roll up, get your tickets here.

Miss Fotherington, a prim English woman, bustles in down the street

Barnum hands her a playbill

Miss Fotherington Oh, thank you very much. It sounds most exciting! (*She drops her handkerchief*)

Passepartout Excuse me, mademoiselle, you have dropped your handkerchief.

Miss Fotherington Thank you, sir, how nice it is to hear the Queen's English again. I do so love the dear Chinese but I get terribly muddled with their language.

Passepartout But we are in Hong Kong, mademoiselle, it is we who must sound muddled.

Miss Fotherington I suppose so. How I long for dear old Battersea Park.

Passepartout How long are you staying in China?

Miss Fotherington Well, I leave tonight in fact, but not, alas, for England. I'm involved in various charitable and missionary projects in South East Asia. I have made my rounds of inspections of our interests in Hong Kong and tonight I must sail for Japan.

Passepartout Japan! Tonight! But there must be some mistake. My friends and I missed the steamer to Yokahama yesterday and there isn't another one until noon tomorrow.

Miss Fotherington The Lord's business cannot wait for the vagaries of steamer timetables. Fortunately one of our flock here had access to a boat allowing us to leave tonight.

Passepartout But what an extraordinary stroke of luck. Mademoiselle, I hate to intrude, and please excuse the liberty but I wonder if I might ask you a huge favour?

Miss Fotherington You'd like to travel with us?

Passepartout If it wouldn't be an inconvenience.

Miss Fotherington Well, I gather it's a modest vessel but I'm sure my contact would be happy to help for a small donation to our work in the East.

Passepartout But of course. Although I'm afraid my master's *will* be rather a small donation. Due to a little mix-up back in India we are a bit low on funds.

Miss Fotherington Your master? How many people are there in your party?

Passepartout Well ... My master, Princess Aouda and myself.

Miss Fotherington Royalty! Well, I'm sure I'd be delighted to help. But I'm afraid we only have one free cabin.

Passepartout I shall be happy to make myself a bed in one of the lifeboats.
Miss Fotherington How enterprising of you. Well, then it is settled. Do tell their highnesses that we sail from the West Quay at dusk.

Miss Fotherington exits

Passepartout What a wonderful stroke of luck! All will be well! If we leave tonight we may get back on schedule. I will tell Monsieur Fogg the moment he wakes from his afternoon nap. It's so simple. What could possibly go wrong?

SCENE 4

Captain Fix enters

Fix Hallo again, little French person.
Passepartout Oh, no! No! It's Monsieur Bang Bang! You got me into big trouble before, monsieur.
Fix (*lying*) My dear fellow, I can't tell you how guilty I was to hear that our little expedition nearly scuppered your round the world adventure. Imagine my relief when I heard that Mr Fogg had managed to buy his way out of that spot of bother.
Passepartout You do not fool me, monsieur. That was a dirty trick. I know you have bet your money on us failing. Well I'll have you know that I, Passepartout, have saved the day once again. I have found us a passage on a missionary lady boat that will take us to Japan in time to get back on schedule.
Fix I'm very impressed, monsieur. It seems I have underestimated your chances of success and may indeed have lost my wager. The best man has won. (*He pauses. He looks sly*) And to show there's no hard feelings, why don't you let me help you celebrate your latest good fortune?
Passepartout Celebrate? But I must tell my master that we sail at dusk.
Fix Dusk? Why, that's hours away. There's plenty of time for me to take you to this very special establishment I know here in Hong Kong.
Passepartout Oh, but I'd better not. I should go. Besides, I saw a pretty ring in the market place. I'd like to buy it for my girl, when I ask her to marry me.
Fix But this place is only around the corner. Here, give this ring to your girlfriend. I don't need it. (*He hands Passepartout a ring*)
Passepartout But I couldn't accept such a beautiful, valuable ——
Fix I want to make up for that little unpleasantness with the cow. I know you'll love it at Mrs Chang's. Very few tourists have the pleasure. It's only for visitors of real discernment. A gentleman of your obvious intelligence, I know you'd feel right at home.

Passepartout You're very kind, monsieur, but I think I should ——
Fix Now let's not hear another word. It's only round the corner. Down that
little alleyway there.

*A door at the back of the set opens. Smoke and red light spill out. It looks
scary. Music begins*

Passepartout But, it looks very dark and gloomy down there. (*He puts the
ring in his pocket*)
Fix Ah!, you see that's to keep out the riff-raff. It's very exclusive but I know
Mrs Chang's going to love you to bits. (*He sings*)

No. 12 The Luxuriant Brew

> Don't be shy
> Step this way
> There's a little joint I know.
> Till you've tried
> What's inside
> I can't let you go.
> Other tourist trips are phoney, come
> Fly the city's pandemonium
> Try some class "A" Chinese opium
> Come on, boy, let's blow.

The Lights change to indicate the inside of an opium den

*Opium Sellers, including Mrs Chang, come out of the smoke. They carry
big oriental cushions for Passepartout and Fix to sit on. They also carry
a hookah used to smoke opium*

Passepartout Opium. I never tried it. Will I need my chopsticks? (*He pulls
some chopsticks out of his pocket*)
Fix I don't think so.

> (*Singing*)   Just listen to me friend
>   I'll show you the score
>   One taste of this pleasure
>   You'll be begging for more.

Mrs Chang steps forward

Mrs Chang   Well, well hallo there, Captain Fix,
                   You've come back to us

	We've been so sad without you
	And look, you've brought along
	A new friend to play with us
Fix	Yes, and you know what to do.

The Opium Sellers surround Passepartout and start to massage him. Passepartout likes this

Opium Sellers	Welcome here,
	Honoured guests,
	We can bring you ecstasy
	You'll forget all your cares
	We can set your spirit free
	There's no pleasure that we don't allow.

| **Fix** | Let's forget the business with the cow. |
| **Opium Sellers** | Just lie back and smoke our hookah now. |

There is suspense. Will he take a puff? No

| **Passepartout** | P'raps a cup of tea. |

The Opium Sellers huddle together to discuss what to do. Fix storms over to them and grabs the hookah

Fix *(speaking; agressively to the Sellers)* Give it to me! *(All smiles, he turns back to Passepartout)*

(Singing)	No need to be scared, lad,
	Relax you're in luck
	You just need to trust me
	Pucker up there and suck.
Fix **OpiumSellers** }	Come on, allow yourself a taste of the Orient
	Inhale the luxuriant brew.
	Why let the native fellows have all the fun of this
	Feel its seductive kiss too.

Passepartout finally smokes the opium

Fix	That's it, boy, take it deep
	Go on have another puff
	And again, breathe it in
(He grabs some) God! It's magic stuff.
	Have some more to waste it's criminal

Passepartout   Well it's certainly original
                      I think it could be medicinal
                      Right, I'd better be off.

Doped, he comes over all "love and peace". He turns to the Opium Sellers

                      I think that I love you
                      And I love you as well
                      And I love this nice lady
                      Now, where is my hotel?

A stoned Passepartout does a funny dance with the Opium Sellers

Fix   So, my friend,
                      Got you now
                      You're not going back to town.
                      Fogg won't hear
                      There's a boat
                      Now you're doped, you clown.
                      God, I'm clever, drink your fill of me
                      Six foot three of total villainy (*Change height reference
                      as appropriate to the actor playing Fix*)
                      What's that brimstone smell?
                      Well hell it's me!

Passepartout sways, staring blankly into space

                      Perhaps you'd better lie down!

On the final beat of the song, he gives the rigid Passepartout a little tap

   Passepartout falls backwards and is carried off by the Opium Sellers

Fix laughs nastily

Music underscoring (**No 12a**)

The Lights dim as the setting is rearranged for the following scene

A spotlight comes up on a suitcase, which opens to reveal a pop-up Japanese scene

Announcer (*voice only*) Fifteenth November! Forty Days to go!

SCENE 5

The Lights come up on the deck of a Chinese Junk. Stars light up at the back of the set

Miss Fotherington appears on a top level with a telescope. Three Chinese sailors sit cross-legged and asleep, their faces hidden beneath coolie hats

Miss Fotherington Splice the mainsails, me hearties, shiver me timbers and throw me over the yardarm, with a yo ho ho and a lovely cup of Earl Grey. What splendid fun.

Fogg and Aouda appear on the deck below. Aouda is furious with Fogg

Aouda I don't know how you can just leave Passepartout behind like that.
Fogg I assumed he'd be aboard. Miss Fotherington told us she'd met him in the street. Odd he didn't tell us of her invitation to sail for Japan. But still, we bumped into her at the hotel and she invited us herself, so no harm done.
Aouda How can you say that?
Fogg Passepartout is a very resourceful fellow. I'm sure he'll catch up with us.
Aouda And how precisely is he to do that? He's left behind in Hong Kong with no money and no way of following us.
Fogg I trust you're not suggesting we could have passed up this opportunity to get back on schedule?
Aouda I am suggesting exactly that. There are more important things than you winning this ridiculous wager.
Fogg Madam, a wager is never ridiculous to an Englishman.

Aouda gasps with exasperation

Aouda Why you pig-headed ... Don't you have any qualms about just abandoning him like that?
Fogg Of course. I'm not totally without feeling
Aouda At last we're getting somewhere.
Fogg Since his utterly selfish disappearance I have been completely unable to locate my pearl cufflinks.
Aouda Well, why don't I have a look for them?
Fogg How kind.
Aouda And then if I find them I can ram them down your ungrateful throat.

Miss Fotherington calls down to them

Miss Fotherington Cooo-eee! Your Highness, is everything satisfactory?

Aouda (*all smiles*) Quite. Thank you, Miss Fotherington.

Miss Fotherington Oh do call me Patricia.

Aouda And you must call me Aouda.

Miss Fotherington Oh, good heavens, your Highness. I couldn't possibly. Isn't it a wonderful view this evening? The moon reflected in the calm rippling waves. So romantic. Just the thing for you honeymooning lovebirds.

Aouda (*to Fogg*) And that's another thing!

Miss Fotherington I hope you don't mind if I join you for a moment.

She exits from the top level in order to climb down

Fogg There was only one cabin left. She simply assumed we were married. I had to go along with it or she would never have taken us along.

Aouda If you imagine for a moment that I'm sharing that tiny cabin with you ...

Fogg I shall of course sleep on deck. Where perhaps I'll get a little peace and quiet.

Aouda Perhaps. Although I'm sure the seagulls will find your company as provoking as I do.

Miss Fotherington enters

She conducts the three sailors. Softly and in harmony, they hum the traditional Irish folk song "The Water is Wide" whilst the dialogue continues. (**No. 12b**)

Miss Fotherington There they are! Our little pair of cooing turtledoves! I've been teaching some of the sailors a few of our folk songs. Do you know, as soon as I saw the two of you I could tell instantly that you were in love.

Aouda Really?

Fogg How quite, quite extraordinary.

Miss Fotherington Oh, yes. To watch the way the two of you steal little glances at each other when you don't think the other is looking — well, it's quite restored my faith in romance. I was recently cruelly disappointed in love, you know?

Aouda I'm so sorry to hear that.

Miss Fotherington Oh yes. He was a guardsman, you know. A Captain James Fix. I used to call him Fixy.

Fogg How delightful.

Miss Fotherington Everyone warned me he was a cad and a bounder and only after my money but he had such a way with him I was blinded by his charms. He proposed on a beautiful night like this. I was so happy I didn't mind when he said there'd been a mix-up at his bank and he couldn't buy an engagement ring. I offered to wear Mother's if he could get it altered. The next morning he set out with it for the jewellers and I never saw him again. Later that day, I noticed all the charity money for the mission was missing too.

Aouda But that's terrible. Did you tell the police?

Miss Fotherington Oh, I expect I will when I get back to London. But there's a part of me that hopes he'll turn up again and it will all have been a frightful misunderstanding. Am I being naïve do you think?

Aouda Perhaps. A little. But who can say?

Miss Fotherington He certainly never looked at me as your husband looks at you. And here you both are sailing across an enchanted sea to the beautiful city of Yokohama. I think it's one of my favourite places in the world and we're in for a treat. Apparently it's the next stop on Mr Barnum's circus world tour. I hear the elephants are extraordinary. Do you care for the circus, Mr Fogg?

Fogg Not terribly. And I especially don't care for elephants.

Aouda (*bitchily*) I shall make sure Mr Fogg and I have front row seats.

Miss Fotherington How romantic! Aren't you lucky to have such a fine, handsome husband?

Aouda Aren't I.

Miss Fotherington And you, Mr Fogg, to have such a beautiful royal bride. Tell me, was it love at first sight?

Fogg I wouldn't put it quite like that.

Miss Fotherington Won't you please indulge a foolish romantic for a moment and tell me what is it that you love most about this gorgeous creature here?

Fogg Oh, I think we must spare her blushes.

Aouda (*mischievously*) Oh no, no, my darling, I'd like to hear this. Pray do tell.

No 13. What Do I Love?

Fogg (*singing*)   What do I love?
                        What do I love?
                        Well love is not a word we like to ...

Miss Fotherington and Aouda stare at Fogg

                        Well I love ...
                        I love her eyes
                        That's right ... I find
                        When she looks as she does now

Her eyes flash like they're shooting stars
And it's very hard to put her from my mind.
That's what I love,
I think.

The music continues

Miss Fotherington Oh, how wonderful. And you my dear? Which of this
fine gentleman's many, many qualities do you love the most?
Aouda Me? I ...
(*Singing*)   What do I love?
What do I love?
Well love is not a word we like to ...
Well I love ...
I love his strength
Somehow, he's strong.
When he furrows up his brow
You know he'll never compromise
And he'd carry you if ever things went wrong.
That's what I love,
I think.

The music continues

Miss Fotherington And what have you to say to that, Mr Fogg? What else
makes your heart skip a beat when your beloved is near?

Fogg (*singing*)   What do I love?
What do I love?
Well love is an emotive term and ...
Well I love ...
I love her spark.
There's well — a flame
She's the energy of ten
And the body of an athlete
You only have to meet her once to never be the same
That's what I love.
I think.

Miss Fotherington (*to Aouda*) Now don't tell me you're going to let him
have that last word.

Aouda (*singing*) What do I love?

What do I love?
Well, I wouldn't use the term myself I ...
Well, I love ...
I love his mouth
Somehow his mouth, even when he's wrong
And he's talking rubbish out of it
There's something rather ... I don't know ...
Well, nice about his mouth.
That's what I love.
I think.

The music continues

Miss Fotherington Now, I'm going to be a little mischievous here. If there was one tiny, tiny little thing you could change about each other. What would it be?

Fogg Oh, I'm quite sure I can think of nothing.

Aouda Darling! I shall be sure to remember that and we can chatter about it at every conceivable opportunity.

Fogg And certainly no-one can find as many opportunities for chatter as you, my love.

(*Singing*)	What would I fault?
Aouda	What would I fault?
Both	Well, fault is an expression which ...
Aouda	I'd fault his sulk
Fogg	I'd fault her moods
Aouda	I hate the way he's so damn picky with his foods
Fogg	I hate her noise
Aouda	I hate his calm
Fogg	I hate her constant state of crisis and alarm
Aouda	I hate his taste
Fogg	I hate her style
Aouda	I hate the fact that he will never crack a smile
	I hate that sigh
Fogg	I hate her sniff
Aouda	I hate the way he stands so formal and so stiff
Fogg	I hate her slouch
Aouda	I hate his walk
Fogg	I hate her irritating, shrill excited squawks
Aouda	I hate his books
Fogg	Her little looks
Aouda	His playing cards

Fogg	Her looking-glass
Aouda	His fountain pen
Fogg	Her mother hen
Aouda	His sneezes
Fogg	Her wheezes
Aouda	His cheeses
Fogg	Her freezes
Both (*fiercely*)	That's what I hate.

(*Sweetly – uncertainty creeping in*) I think!

Miss Fotherington Oh, how delightful. Fixy and I used to have our funny little squabbles all the time. Well, I shall leave you cupids to the fun part; the making up! I don't know how I shall sleep, I really don't. I'm so excited about the circus. I'm sure my head will be quite full of dancing elephants. Good-night.

Music undercoring (**No.13b**)

Fogg and Aouda say their good-nights to Miss Fotherington

Miss Fotherington exits

There is a romantic tension between Fogg and Aouda. But neither of them will show what they feel about each other

The Sailors gently hum "The Water is Wide"

Fogg Well, I suppose I should find a berth for the night. I'm told one can make oneself a quite comfortable bed in a lifeboat.

Aouda I've heard that too.

Fogg Well, I shall bid you good-night then.

Aouda Good-night.

Fogg I wonder if I might make so bold ...

Aouda Yes, Mr Fogg?

Fogg Should the wind take a more northerly course during the night and prove somewhat fresher, I wonder if I might ——

Aouda You may knock on the cabin door for an extra blanket.

Fogg Thank you. I should be much obliged.

Aouda Please, don't mention it. (*Beat*) Mr Fogg.

Fogg Yes, your Highness?

Aouda I really am most grateful that you're letting me travel on with you to England.

Fogg Well, may I once again express my deepest sympathies for the death of your uncle in Hong Kong.

Aouda Thank you.
Fogg Good-night then, your Highness.
Aouda Good-night, Mr Fogg.

Fogg exits

Aouda stares out to "sea"

Oh, Passepartout. How will you ever get to Japan?

Black-out

Aouda exits

SCENE 6

*Circus music plays (**No. 14**). Bright Lights come up*

Clowns/Puppeteers burst on to the stage. In amongst them is Barnum, the American ring master

Barnum People of Yokohama! Phineas T. Barnum is proud to bring the good wishes of the American people to you, the people of Japan, as part of our grand world tour. And as a special treat in honour of our visit here today, we are proud to present to you the world première of a brand new act the like of which has never been seen before in any of the far corners of the earth. Ladies and Gentlemen, please welcome on stage — Passepartout and friend!

He exits

Passepartout, dressed in Japanese costume, enters. He pretends to be sad, as if he as lost his elephant friend. He shows around a picture of the animal

No-one recognizes the picture

Eugene, the elephant, walks up behind Passepartout and taps him on the shoulder. The elephant puppet is operated by the clowns

They are happily reunited

Passepartout reprises "Jungle Honeymoon" in cod Japanese, whilst he and Eugene do a dance routine

There is the sound effect of tremendous applause

The Clowns take the elephant off

SCENE 7

The Lights come up on Passepartout. He is backstage of the circus and is talking as if to Eugene, the elephant. The elephant is off stage

Passepartout No, no, Eugene, it's no use getting uppity with me. I think you'll find it's step, ball, change, flick, step, *step*, kick. There's no shuffle, hop, flick.

Aouda and Fogg burst in

Passepartout is delighted to see them

Aouda Passepartout!
Passepartout Your Majesty! Master! I knew you would find us! (*Calling off*) Eugene, look who it is in our dressing-room.

There is the sound effect of an elephant trumpet

Master, can you believe my luck, I applied for a job cleaning out the elephants on Mr Barnum's circus boat and guess who they'd brought from India? Eugene! Come and say hallo, Eugene!

There is the sound effect of an elephant trumpet. The elephant is apparently not interested

Oh, please yourself. He is having a tantrum over a slight artistic difference. I can do nothing with him.
Aouda Both of you were wonderful out there.

Passepartout simpers shyly

Passepartout (*blurting out, excitedly*) I know! But I can't believe you are here. I asked all over Yokohama for you. I'm sorry I got left behind, you see I met the same man who caused all the bang, bang, moo. (*He mimes a cow dying and the Indians screaming, etc.*) But this time he made me go to ——
Fogg Yes, yes, never mind about that now. If we rush we can catch the ten o'clock sailing to America. With the tides in our favour, it will mean we shall arrive a mere sixteen hours behind schedule. Then, if the trains run according to Bradshaw's, there's every chance we can make up for lost

time and get back on course to win the bet. But we must leave now.

Aouda Perhaps Passepartout likes it here.

Passepartout *Non, non*, master. I'm coming. I'm so happy. I never thought I'd see you again. (*Pointedly so Eugene, the elephant, can hear*) Besides, I have had quite enough of show business and diva elephants.

There is the sound of Eugene trumpeting indignantly

But I must go and make reservations for the boat.

Aouda All taken care of. A nice missionary lady has organized our tickets along with hers.

Passepartout Everything is going our way now! We can win the bet and Katy will marry me and everything will be all right.

Barnum bursts in

Barnum Kid, you and the elephant were fantastic. I'm going to make you a star across five continents.

Passepartout You're very kind, monsieur, but I'm afraid I have a prior engagement back in England at precisely twenty-one hundred hours Greenwich Meantime on Christmas Day.

Barnum That's the most ridiculous thing I've ever heard. You'll never make it. Why, if I were a betting man ...

Passepartout Monsieur, if you were a betting man you'd lose your money. We are going to make it!

Barnum Well, actually I *was* thinking the act might work even better with a bearded lady.

Passepartout Eugene will shine whoever is in the supporting cast.

Barnum Kid, that elephant has got star quality. I think you're right.

Fogg We must go.

Passepartout But of course, master. (*To Barnum*) Say goodbye to Eugene for me when he stops sulking. Tell him I shall write.

Barnum Best of luck to you all.

Barnum exits

Fogg So the world's next great continent awaits us and not a moment too soon. I hear there are card players there with an appetite for gambling and I urgently need to replenish our diminished funds.

Passepartout What are we waiting for? America here we come!

*There is a burst of music (**No.15**)*

A suitcase opens to reveal a pop-up buffalo

SCENE 8

The Company enter and fill up the stage as if it were a Wild West saloon.
There are Cowboys and a Saloon Hostess. A Cowboy sits playing at a piano.
There are some mean-looking Gamblers playing poker at a card table in the
corner

The evil-looking cowboy Jesse James arrives

Everyone falls into a frightened silence; the piano playing halts. Jesse takes
his place at the poker table and then signals that everyone should go about
their business

The piano starts up again

The music stops, the lighting dims and the saloon freezes

A Spotlight comes up on Passepartout as he enters. He writes a letter to Katy

Passepartout (*as he writes*) "My darling Katy, so here we are in the Wild
West of America on the last big stage of our journey. Princess Aouda and
Miss Fotherington are advising the sheriff on the advantages of implementing
a clear municipal public health policy and Mr Fogg is trying to win us some
money for train tickets from some poker players."

The saloon comes to life once more

Fogg enters

The Lights come up as Fogg arrives at the card table

Fogg Gentleman, it's your lucky day. Allow me to introduce you to the
riveting intellectual challenge that is "whist".
Everyone (*mystified*) Whist?

The action freezes, the Lights dim and the Spotlight returns to Passepartout

Passepartout (*as he writes*) "I have had many, many adventures to make you
laugh — and sometimes despair of me, but Mr Fogg says we can still win
the wager so I want you to book your ticket to meet me at nine o'clock, at
Greenwich, England on Christmas Day when we will be big, big heroes
and — (*he takes out Fix's ring*) and I have a big, big surprise for you.

A saloon singer, Tammy Lou enters, wearing a stars and stripes outfit.
Tammy Lou is played by the same actress who plays Katy in Act I

"Oh, Katy, as we get closer to the finish, I can't help thinking about you all the time. Almost everything we see in this big, strange country reminds me of you."

The Lights come up. The saloon comes to life and the Saloon Hostess moves C

Saloon Hostess (*announcing*) Now, settle down, you varmints! And give a nice Deadman's Creek welcome to some great dames of the Great Plains. Tammy Lou's Around-the-States revue. (*She moves away*)

Bearing an uncanny resemblance to Katy's dance troupe in Act I, the Show girls enter and move C. *However, this time the girls wear frocks covered in stars and stripes*

Tammy Lou moves C

They sing

No. 16 Around the States with Tammy's Dames

Tammy Lou	From Delaware to Albuquerque
Show Girls	My gals sure are talking turkey
	"Round the States with Tammy's Dames",
	President Ulysses Simpson Grant says
	We enchant him during Congress
	"Round the States with Tammy's Dames ".

The music continues. They dance throughout the following. Tammy notices Passepartout gazing mournfully at the routine

Tammy Lou (*dancing*) Hey partner, you OK? You're looking kind of blue.
Passepartout *Pardon,* mademoiselle. I'm just homesick for my baby.
Tammy Lou Girls, looks like this one-horse town's got itself another lonesome cowboy. (*To the band*) Hit it! Two-three-four!

They sing

Tammy Lou	From Delaware to Albuquerque
Show Girls	My gals sure are talking turkey
	"Round the States with Tammy's Dames",
	President Ulysses Simpson Grant says
	We enchant him during Congress
	"Round the States with Tammy's Dames ".

The dance is interrupted by a commotion in the corner around Fogg and the card game

Jesse James Say, what is this whist! I knew we should have stuck to poker. That's a pretty long winning streak you've been enjoying, mister. Boys, I think this guy's been trying to make a fool out of Jesse James.

Fogg My dear Mr James, whist is simply a matter of applying a numeric logic allied to any given sequence of chance. If you're interested, I'd be happy to show you the system of applied thinking as devised by my friend Septimus Greeb and expanded in last September's Journal of Modern Thought.

Jesse James (*with a hand on his holster*) And I'd be happy to show you how we deal with swizzlers around these parts.

The crowd gather, in horror, by the exit. Members of James's gang gather to back him up

Fogg My dear sir, I should warn you that if you're calling me a cheat then I shall be forced to accept your challenge to a duel.

All the Americans, apart from the Hostess and James and his gang, scream and exit

It is only fair, however, that you should know I held the Queensberry title for amateur shooting for five years.

Jesse James I'm quaking in my boots.

The Hostess approaches Passepartout

Hostess (*to Passepartout*) You'd better get your friend out of here. I ain't never seen anyone walk away alive once Jesse's had a mind to put a bullet in them.

Fogg I'm afraid I cannot fight you just at the moment as I am engaged upon winning a wager. Something that you as a gambling man will understand, I'm sure. However, if you'd like to get out your diary I'm sure we can find a mutually convenient time for me to return to America and conclude our business.

Jesse James Are you trying to make a jackass out of me, mister? Why, I'm going to shoot you so full of holes you'll fall to pieces.

To distract James and his gang, the Hostess fires some shots into the air

What the devil was that?

Cowboy I bet you it's that McGregor gang again. Didn't we teach them a lesson the last time?

Jesse James We'd better show 'em who's in charge round here once and for all.

The Cowboys rush out

The Hostess bundles Passepartout and Fogg towards another exit

Saloon Hostess You'd better make yourself scarce whilst they're distracted. I don't want my bar shot to pieces again.

Fogg (*to the Hostess*) Perhaps you'd pass on my compliments to Mr Jesse James who has accused me of cheating. (*He consults his diary*)

Passepartout scoops up Fogg's winnings into his carpet-bag from the card table

Passepartout This should make up for the money we lost in India.

Fogg Could you please tell him that, if quite convenient, February seventeenth would seem an ideal date for me to return and settle the matter.

Saloon Hostess Just get out of here.

Black-out

<h2 align="center">Scene 9</h2>

There is blast of train sound effects

The Lights come up on Fogg, Passepartout, Aouda and Miss Fotherington with other fellow travellers as they mill around a rural station platform. There is a Union Pacific Station Guard and Farmer Hitch. Some of the crowd will turn out to be Hitch's Mormon Wives

During the following, Hitch stops to listen into the conversation

Fogg stops the Union Pacific Station Guard

Fogg Excuse me, my good man, can you tell us the name of this station and why we've been advised to alight here?

Union Pacific Guard Why this is Salt Lake, sir, and it looks like we're stuck here for a while. There's a problem on the track ahead.

Passepartout But we are in a hurry, monsieur. We have to catch our boat in New York. The train always moves so slowly.

Union Pacific Guard The track ain't even in these parts; last month Jesse James and his gang tried to derail then rob the mail train.

Fogg And the problem ahead?

Union Pacific Guard Buffalo on the line.

Fogg Well, we might as well have a look around. Salt Lake is a settlement established by a religious sect whose unconventional beliefs are causing much controversy across America, particularly concerning their domestic arrangements.

Hitch Ain't that the truth, brother, but we'll win them around to our way of thinking about running the homestead.

Aouda What is that precisely?

Hitch Well, if you've got some time, strangers, settle down and I'll tell you all about it. I think you gentlemen will find this this an inspirational story. (*He sings in the style of an evangelist preacher*)

No. 17 Life Here in the Wilderness

Life here in the wilderness is very, very hard
A man could go quite crazy with the toil

A Wife runs to his side

My wife and I we laboured long
From dawn to dust we strived
But still we got no mercy from the soil.
I prayed me to Jesus
Said, "Lord, what will I do?"
There's simply too much work for only two.
And the answer came back "advertise".
I said, "I can't afford no hired guys",
And then I realized what I had to do.

The Mormon Women sing all the yeah, yeah, yeahs. During the following, the song gets more infectious. It growing bigger and bigger in its evangelical style

A second Wife joins in

	Get another wife.
Women	Yeah! Yeah!
Hitch	An extra wife
Women	Yeah! Yeah!
Hitch	A brand new wife
Women	Yeah!

Hitch	Wife
Women	Yeah!
Hitch	Treatin' me nice.

Matrimony's running rife
So up your dose of trouble and strife
Let a brand new lady in your life
Go grab another wife.

Took an advertisement out to find an extra hand
Those ladies beat a path clean to my door
Chose a buxom gal with milking hands

A third Wife joins

And that worked out real fine
Milk and honey soon began to pour.
So I bought out my neighbour
But soon I came to see
There was too much work for only three
The preacher said that I should get
Some hired hands, I said not yet,
That's big of you but I got bigamy.

Miss Fotherington and Passepartout find themselves caught up in the routine, despite the efforts of Aouda and Fogg to restrain them

More Wives join Hitch

	Get another wife
Women	Yeah! Yeah!
Hitch	An extra wife
Women	Yeah! Yeah!
Hitch	A brand new wife
Women	Yeah!
Hitch	Wife
Women	Yeah!
Hitch	Treatin' me nice.
	Matrimony's running rife
	So up your dose of trouble and strife
All	Let a brand new lady in your life
	Go grab another wife.

Jesse James's gang enters, wearing cloaks and bonnets, disguised as Mormon Wives. They join in with the routine

Hitch	That was seven years ago, I haven't looked back yet.
	I've marched half Northern Utah down the aisle
	But I keep finding vacancies
	That's why I need you gals, you see
	So role your sleeves up, make your hubby smile.
	Got a wife to wash the dishes
	Got a wife to buy the seeds
	Got a wife to sew, got a wife to reap
	And a wife to clear the weeds.
	Got a wife to go to market
Women	Yeah!
Hitch	Got a wife to feed the sow
Women	Yeah!
Hitch	Got a wife for milking, wife for chickens
	Wife to mend the plough.
All	Got a wife
Hitch	To do the baking
All	Got a wife
Hitch	To sweep the path
All	Got a wife
Hitch	To dust,
All	A wife
Hitch	To paint,
All	And a wife
Hitch	To run the bath.
Women	Yeah!
All	Got a wife
Hitch	To do my boots up
All	Got a wife
Hitch	To make 'em shine.
Women	Yeah! (Yeah! yeah!)
Hitch	Got a wife to clean my dirty shirts
	Then hang 'em on the line.
Women	Yeah!
Hitch	Now, see I've made you jealous,
	You're disappointed too.
	But since I'm such a loving man,
	I'll tell you what I'll do.
	Get another wife
Women	Another wife

A Preacher and a New Bride in a veil enters. She has a sign around her neck reading "Just arrived"

Hitch welcomes her

Hitch	An extra wife
Women	An extra wife
Hitch	A brand new wife
Women	Yeah!
Hitch	Wife
Women	Yeah! Yeah!
Hitch	Treatin' me nice.
All	Matrimony's running rife,
	So up your dose of trouble and strife.
	Let a brand new lady in your life,
	Go grab another wife.

The last verse is repeated with a huge finish

As the applause dies down, Jesse James enters and shoots into the air for silence

Jesse James (*to Fogg*) So, Englishman, we catch up with you at last. We had to ride hard but I don't let nobody make a fool out of Jesse James.

James's gang rip off their disguises. The Wives scream

Now where's the money you fleeced from me at cards? And the rest of you. Empty your pockets!

Hitch Don't hurt me, sir. I've got twenty-two wives to support. Here, why don't you-all take a few? I got 'em to spare. They all got their own teeth.

The Wives all panic. Aouda grabs a gun from one of the gang and strides C. *She fires it into the air to get everyone's attention*

Aouda Ladies, I've had just about enough of this. Ever since I started my travels men have pushed me around. My husband wanted to take me to the grave with him, like some possession, along with the funeral sweetmeats and his favourite dog. This man —— (*she points the gun at Hitch*)

Everyone ducks

— enslaves you all to toil on his farm for the rest of your lives and now more men want to push us around. Well I say enough is enough. We deserve more respect. We're better than this. Now, are we going to wait around for one of our lords and masters to protect us from these bandits, or are we going to stand up for ourselves? Get them!

The following is underscored. (**No. 18**) *The Women fight the bandits. Aouda is particularly impressive at kick-boxing*

The fight continues during the following in slow motion

Hitch (*of Aouda*) Wow, she sure is something special.
Fogg She certainly is.
Hitch You're going to have your work cut out married to that polecat.
Fogg Oh, she's not my wife ... She ... There's some mistake.
Hitch Whatever you say, brother!

The fight comes back to life. During this fight, Passepartout drops his ring. He stops the fight

Passepartout Stop! Stop! I'm sorry to be a nuisance, every one, but I think I've dropped the engagement ring I was going to give to my girl.

Everyone stops and looks. A particularly Mean Bandit finds it

Mean Bandit Is this it?
Passepartout Thank you, monsieur.

The Mean Bandit turns out to be a softy

Mean Bandit (*softly*) It sure is purdy (*pretty*).
Passepartout Do you think so? Do you think she'll like it?

All the women and the Mean Bandit go all girly and forget the fight. They gather excitedly around the ring to the bemusement of the other bandits. Fogg tries to fight his way out of the scrum

   Jesse James, his bad gang members and Hitch sneak off

Passepartout is chattering away. The girls squeal their delight

Passepartout I was thinking about a May wedding. I know it's a cliché but — Paris in the spring time! But, then I'm also thinking, "Why wait?"

There is the sound of a train leaving. Fogg finally makes himself heard above the noise

Fogg The bandits have stolen the train.

The Mean Bandit runs towards the exit

Mean Bandit Hey! Wait for me.

He exits

Silence. The wind begins to whistle around them

Miss Fotherington There's a strong north wind blowing too. It looks like it's going to snow.
Announcer (*in a worried voice*) Seventh December. Eighteen days left!
Fogg Confound it! We'll never make New York in time to sail to Liverpool now.
Aouda Oh, yes, we will. There's a broken trolley car in that siding. We can fix a mast to it. We'll sew our undergarments together into some kind of a sail to catch that north wind. Ladies, knickers off!

*Music underscoring (**No. 19**)*

The Lights change as they form themselves into a tableau. They rearrange props for a railway truck and cling to it, bending forward as if the trolley car is speeding

Scene 10

A Spotlight comes up on Queen Victoria and Disraeli as they enter

Disraeli Extraordinary news, Marm. Phileas Fogg is speeding across the American plains in a sail-powered open railway truck with a troop of half-naked Mormon wives!
Queen Victoria (*steely*) How many half-naked Mormon wives?
Disraeli About ten, your Majesty.
Queen Victoria Good heavens! What would my poor Albert have made of it all?
Disraeli I suspect he would have recommended Mr Fogg for a knighthood, Marm.

They exit

The Lights come up and the trolley car tableau comes to life. Everyone clambers off, rushing towards the exit behind Fogg

Fogg leads the way

Fogg This way to our next train!

They exit. Holmes and Watson enter

Dr Watson Holmes! Holmes! Have you seen this morning's *Times*? It seems Fogg has managed to catch a train in Omaha. At this rate he may get back on target.
Sherlock Holmes How splendid. As a special treat, Watson, I shall let you do the crossword.

They exit

The Lights change and there is the sound of a train screeching to a halt

Passengers enter and gather around a Guard. Fogg enters and approaches the Guard. The Guard is cowardly

Fogg What seems to be the trouble here?
Guard It's the bridge ahead, sir. It's been damaged in a storm. I don't think it'll take the weight of the train.
Fogg Nonsense, shovel some more coal in and let's run the bridge at full speed. What's the matter with you? Are we men or are we mice?

Everyone rushes off

A little model train runs along the top of the set. A section of the set collapses after the train has passed over

A Spotlight comes up on Disraeli and Victoria as they enter

Disraeli He's not going to make it, Marm. The boat he's requisitioned to cross the Atlantic can't carry enough fuel to travel the distance with sufficient speed!

The Spotlight cross-fades to Fogg as he enters

There is noise of hammering and sawing

Fogg Rip up the decking, rip out the cabins, tear up anything that can be burnt and throw it into the furnace to power the ship. We have to make it to Liverpool in time for the London train or all is lost.

He exits

As Fogg exits the Spotlight cross-fades back to Queen Victoria and Disaeli

Queen Victoria My smelling salts if you please, Mr Disraeli. All this excitement is giving me palpitations.

They exit

Sherlock Holmes and Dr Watson enter into the Spotlight

Someone rushes across the stage in a panic and announces to the audience

Announcer One day left!
Sherlock Holmes I'm sure they'll find the Liverpool cab drivers well up to the task.

Sherlock Holmes and Dr Watson exit

The Lights change

SCENE 11

There are station noises

Fogg, Passepartout, Miss Fotherington and Aouda run on breathless and clutching their luggage. This includes the carpet-bag of money. The mood is tense

Fogg Two minutes to spare.
Miss Fotherington Well, good luck everyone, I must attend to my business in Liverpool. It's been the most exciting few weeks of my life.

Fogg kisses her hand

I hope to read in the paper that you've won your wager -- even if you aren't actually married! Yet!

A Porter enters. Mrs Fotherington exits

Fogg (*approaching the Porter*) Excuse me, can you tell me which is the
London train?

The Porter points

Passepartout Hurry, everyone.

They start to cross the stage

  *A Detective and Policeman step into their path. The have Liverpudlian
  accents*

Detective Mr Phileas Fogg?
Fogg Yes?
Detective Mr Jean Passepartout?
Passepartout *Oui*, monsieur.
Detective I must ask you both to come with me please; you're under arrest.
  We received a telegram from a Captain Fix detailing some very serious
  allegations that must be investigated.

*As the Detective continues, the Policeman inspects the carpet-bag full of
money that Fogg won gambling in the Wild West saloon*

  I'm arresting you for the theft of an antique engagement ring and the funds
  of the Battersea Park missionary foundation.
Fogg I'm sorry, detective, there must be some mistake. I've never even heard
  of the foundation.
Policeman Look at this, sir, a bag full of American money.
Detective That makes sense. The foundation lost donations to its work from
  all over the world. If you two gentlemen would like to accompany me to
  the station we can search you for the stolen ring.

Passepartout hands over Fix's ring

Passeparout Would this be the ring, monsieur?
Detective It certainly fits the description.
Passepartout (*urgently*) But Mr Fogg won the money playing with with
  Wild West poker players and I was given the ring in Hong Kong outside
  a den of —(*he mimes taking opium and hallucinating*) suck, suck — woo,
  woo.

The Detective takes out a notebook

Detective (*writing*) "Suck, suck, woo, woo" . That'll be your defence will it,
  sir?

Aouda Just a minute. That foundation? Isn't that Miss Fotherington's charity and didn't she once tell us that she'd had a ring stolen?

There is the sound of a train departing

Fogg What does it matter? We've missed the train, I've lost everything. Everything that matters to me. I'm a failure. Well, I deserve it. I thought I was so clever, but I made so many stupid mistakes. I should have foreseen the buffalo on the track on the Great Plains. Known that the Indian railway didn't run as far as Allahabad. In fact we could have avoided that country all together and saved three days. India was a complete waste of time.

Reacting to Fogg, Aouda drops what she is holding and runs off in distress

Fogg What on earth is the matter with ... (*Realizing what he has said*) Oh, wait! Of course I didn't mean ...

But she's gone

Detective Come along, gentlemen.

Passepartout and Fogg are escorted off by the Policeman and Detective

*The Lights change. Music underscoring (**No. 19b**)*

Scene 12

Aouda runs to the "water's edge" of Liverpool's dock. Some distance away another woman enters, a Sailor's Wife. She looks out into the "water", waiting for her man to return

There are stars

Sailor's Wife Careful down by the water's edge, love, it's deep and the pier's slippy down there.

Aouda is preoccupied

No. 20 How was I to Know

Aouda How was I to know I loved him?
When he said those things
It chilled me to the bone
The last thing I need now
Is to nurse a broken heart
I'd have run for cover if I'd only known.

> If I'd seen the signs
> But I never missed him before now
> So I was blind
> Not to have kissed him before now.
>
> I am not a foolish woman
> I am not a little girl.
> So when he said those words
> Why did my world start to unfurl?
> There's no problem, I'll forget him.
> So what's a little pain?
> My only worry's that my world
> Can never be the same.

The other woman hums gently as Aouda gazes out over the "water"

On another part of the stage, a Spotlight comes up on Fogg and Passepartout being released from prison by the Liverpudlian Detective

Detective Mr Fogg, my sincere apologies for the mix-up. I hope your cell wasn't too draughty.

Passepartout Hurry, master, you have to find her and tell her you didn't mean what you said. I've never seen her so upset. I'm very worried about her. Hurry, please.

Fogg But what will I say ... What if I can't find the words?

Passepartout You'll think of something. Please go before anything bad happens to her.

Detective This is a bad business, a bad business, that's for sure.

The Detective exits

The Lights go down on Fogg and Passepartout

They exit

Other Wives enter and join Aouda, to wait for their husbands. They carry lanterns

Aouda contemplates throwing herself into the water

Aouda (*singing*) And what's left for me now
> Without a home, without this man?
> With no-one I can turn to,
> With answer or no plan?

The Wives sing softly

Wives   For love is gentle
          And love is fine
          The sweetest flower
          When first it's new
          But love grows old
          And waxes cold
          And fades away
          Like morning dew.

One by one their men, Sailors carrying kitbags, enter and embrace their Wives

The couples sing across Aouda

Aouda   How was I to know I loved him?
          And now there's no turning back
          Where's my famous resolution
          Where's the dignity I lack?

Couples   The water is wide
          I can't cross over
          And neither have
          I wings to fly ...

Aouda   Let's bring the curtain down
          Upon my squalid little tale
          Another heroine
          Who lost the plot and left the rails ...

Couples   Give me a boat
          That can carry two...

Aouda It's funny standing here now   **Couples** And both shall row
       When my life's up in the air   My love and I.
       But the truth is if I end things
       I know he wouldn't even care.

The couples leave

Fogg pushes through them to get to Aouda

SCENE 13

The action immediately follows with no break

Fogg There you are. I've been looking for you all over Liverpool. Thank you
for sending Miss Fotherington to sort out that business with the police. It
was her engagement ring. Very clever of you.
Aouda Thank you. Now, I wonder if you'd leave me alone now, please.
Fogg But, Aouda, it's freezing out here. What are you doing down here by
the water? (*Realizing she's considering suicide*) Oh, no, Aouda.

Music underscore (**No. 20a**)

Aouda No doubt you think I'm a very foolish woman. I have feelings and
I have a heart and whether I like it or not, that heart has been broken by you,
Mr Fogg. But it is not your fault. You didn't ask for any of this and I do not
expect you to understand. Perhaps you'll go now and leave me to my fate.
Fogg No, no, I — of course, I understand. You don't know how often I've
looked at you and wanted to tell you that I — admire you — that I ... And
then the business of the wager got in the way and I ... But I never stopped
thinking about you ... I never stopped ... I just can't show you my feelings.
I've never been able to ... Sometimes I look at people falling in love around
me, or crying or even laughing, and I wish I could let go like that to just let
the emotion burst out of me but I lived alone for so long with my schedules
and my timetables that I've even forgotten how to laugh. But it doesn't
mean that I don't have a heart beating inside me.

Christmas bells start to sound

A Passerby enters

Passerby Merry Christmas to you both.
Fogg You're a little late, aren't you, my friend? Christmas Day was
yesterday.
Passerby I hope not, mister. Otherwise there's going to be a lot of plum
pudding eaten today for no good reason. It's December twenty-fifth all
right. You ask my little 'un.

He exits

Fogg and Aouda look at each other

A figure — Fix— enters into the shadows and listens to them

Fogg and Aouda do not notice

Fogg Christmas day? But it can't be. That would mean ...

Aouda Just a minute, how were you gauging our progress during the voyage?

Fogg By my father's watch. (*He takes out a fob watch*) A remarkable instrument. It's never lost a minute in fifty years.

Aouda And did you alter the time when you crossed the time zones?

Fogg What do you mean?

Aouda Surely, Mr Fogg! Schoolboy mathematics.

Music underscoring (**No. 20b**)

By journeying constantly eastward you have been travelling towards the sun gaining four minutes on Greenwich Meantime with every day that you've travelled.

Fogg There are three-hundred and sixty degrees in the circumference of the earth and three-hundred and sixty multiplied by four minutes gives precisely twenty-four hours.

Aouda So whilst you, going East, saw the sun pass the Meridian eighty times, here in England it's only passed it seventy-nine times.

Fogg But that means ... (*He starts to laugh*)

Aouda Mr Fogg.

Fogg Yes?

Aouda You're laughing!

Fogg Yes, yes I am! Everything's going to be all right. (*He stops laughing and looks intently into Aouda's eyes*) I'll make everything all right.

Passepartout arrives out of breath carrying suitcases

Passepartout Master! Master! Guess what!

Fogg
Aouda } (*together; with delight*) We know!

Fogg, Aouda and Passepartout rush off

The music becomes sinister

Fix steps out of the shadows

Fix Well, well, well.

Black-out

He exits

SCENE 14

There is a banner which reads, "Welcome back to Greenwich"

The stage fills with people at Greenwich — including the Mayor and Fix — waiting to see if Fogg will return on time. There are a few carol singers. They sing rather half-heartedly

Katy, carrying her luggage, rushes in

Katy Have I missed it? Have I missed the hero's return? Are they back yet?

The people in the crowd shout out

Voice 1 No, not yet.
Voice 2 They won't be here. The whole thing's ridiculous if you ask me. I'm glad I haven't got money on it.
Voice 3 Well, I have and I think it's safe. That Phileas Fogg's a resourceful fellow.
Katy Well, actually I heard the real brains of the operation is the Frenchman, Jean Passepartout. And I'm going to be his wife — that's if he turns up.

General laughter from the crowd

A church clock starts to chime nine o'clock. Everyone groans and scoffs

The banner falls down at one side

The Mayor steps forward to make a speech

Mayor Well, that's the clock at the Observatory striking nine. I think we have to conclude that Mr Fogg will not be joining us and that the wager is lost.

There is another groan from the crowd

Katy (*calling*) Hold on a minute! It's not nine o'clock until the bells stop chiming. Don't give up yet.

Music underscoring (**No. 20c**)

Fogg, Passepartout and Aouda arrive on time

There is much cheering, hugging and congratulations. Passepartout spots Fix on the edge of the crowd and freezes, staring at him. The crowd sense his mood and the jubilation stops

Passepartout You, monsieur! How dare you show your face here. You tried to ruin everything over and over!

Fix I was simply trying to win my wager. The wager that I placed on your failing the challenge.

Fogg Then I trust, sir, that you have lost a great deal of money.

Fix On the contrary. When the whole time zone mix-up came to my attention I switched the bet and placed all my money on your succeeding. I'm now a very wealthy man.

Miss Fotherington appears behind him

Miss Fotherington (*sweetly*) Fixy!

Fix turns to see her and screams

What wonderful news, Fixy. Now you'll be able to pay back, with interest, all the money you borrowed from my charity and you can jolly well make proper use of this engagement ring, unless you want me to take the whole matter to the police. What do you say, Mr Fogg? Shall we let the whole matter drop if my fiancé pledges himself to marital bliss with me, spreading goodwill and his money around the world.

Fogg I think that sounds most satisfactory. What do you say, Captain Fix?

Fix (*holding out his hand*) Ring!

Miss Fotherington gives him the ring

(*Bitterly*) Miss Fotherington. Would you do me the honour?

Miss Fotherington Of course I will, Fixy.

Everyone cheers

Fixy?

Fix Yes, dear.

Miss Fotherington Shall we go and write some cheques?

Fix (*dejectedly*) Yes, dear.

Everyone laughs as

Miss Fotherington leads Fix off

Passepartout And, Katy, I can't give you a fancy ring this time but look, I've got a curtain ring I pulled off the drapes in the railway carriage. Would you marry me?

Katy Oh, Passepartout! It's the only ring I'll ever want.

There is much crying and hugging, etc. Everyone looks expectantly at Fogg and Aouda

Fogg Right. Well. I think we're finished here. If you'll excuse me, I must retire to the British Library and ... (*Aware that everyone is looking at him and Aouda expectantly he pulls himself together*) Yes, well. From the bottom of my heart. A heart that I have only recently learned to open up to the world. From the bottom of my heart — Princess Aouda, will you do me the honour of being my wife?

There is tension

Aouda Mr Fogg? (*Pause — What will she say?*) Of course I will.

Everyone is delighted

Passepartout Then everything is a happy ending, is it not?
Fogg Yes, Passepartout. Everything is a happy ending.

Fix and Miss Fotherington return as Mr and Mrs Fix

Everyone sings

No. 21 Finale (Passepartout)

All   This time it's gonna be so different to before
                            Goodbye to scraping by
                            So long to being poor.
                            In eighty days we've all come to see ...

Aouda, Katy and Miss Fotherington sing to their men

Aouda   ⎫
Katy   ⎬ There's no reason
Miss Fotherington ⎭ Why you shouldn't be my baby.

Passepartout (*to Katy*) I know I haven't been much of a catch before.
Phileas (*to Aouda*)I know you said you wanted more.
                            So he's changing rearranging
Fix   Rearranging
Passepartout   Look who's made it through.

Everyone lifts Passepartout high as they sing

All   Passepartout
                            Passepartout
                            Passepartout!

Black-out

Music underscoring (**No. 22**)

The Lights come up and the cast take their bows

When everyone is lined up the Company reprise

No. 22 Bows and Finale

(*Singing*)   Everybody dreams of a little adventure
(Close your eyes and dream of adventure)
To feel the sun on your back and the wind in your hair
(Buy a ticket to adventure)
As you're trudging through the day
Living life in shades of grey
Just close your eyes, imagine that you're there.
Anywhere!
Where love and excitement
Wait at the corner
(Close your eyes and dream of adventure)
By a magic lagoon in a tropical haze
(Buy a ticket to the adventure)
There are mountains and a beach
Mighty oceans in your reach
You can get there but...

The big finish

Be home in eighty days!

The Company take their final bows

Music underscoring (**No. 23**) *Play-out*

THE END

FURNITURE AND PROPERTY LIST

ACT I
SCENE 1

Pre-set: Towering stacks of trunks, suitcases, junk
In suitcases: little pop-up Taj Mahal, puppet can-can dancer
Various stage-blocks
Umbrellas
Banner reading "The adventure starts here"

Off stage: Little Union Jack flags (**Cast**)

Personal: **Fogg**: fob-watch

SCENE 2

On stage: *No additional props required*

SCENE 3

On stage: *No additional props required*

SCENE 4

On stage: Make-up

Off stage: Trays and saucepans (**Kitchen staff**)

SCENE 5

On stage: *No additional props required*

Off stage: Luggage (**Company**)
Carpet-bag (**Passepartout**)

Personal: **Railway Porter**: flag, picture

SCENE 6

On stage: No additional props required

Off stage: Laundry/costume with sandbags (**Company**)
               Blue umbrellas painted with clouds (**Company**)
               Puppet birds on sticks (**Company**)

SCENE 7

On stage: No additional props required

Off stage: Model balloon (**Stage-management**)
               Newspaper (**Sherlock Holmes**)
               Postcard (**Katy**)

SCENE 8

On stage: No additional props required

SCENE 9

On stage: Newspaper for **Fix**
               Rifle (optional) for **Fix**

SCENE 10

On stage: No additional props required

Personal: **Fogg**: playing-cards

SCENE 11

On stage: No additional props required

Off stage: Globe (**Queen Victoria**)
               Cup of tea (**Disreali**)

SCENE 12

On stage: Life-sized puppet elephant

SCENE 13

On stage:	*No additional props required*
Off stage:	Shrouded body of the dead Maharaja (**Priests**)

SCENE 14

On stage:	*No additional props required*
Personal:	**Passepartout**: postcard; pen

ACT II
SCENE 1

Pre-set:	Towering stacks of trunks, suitcases, junk *In suitcases*: model of Chinese building; model Japanese scene; pop-up buffalo Various stage-blocks

SCENE 2

On stage:	Chinese banners Chinese dragon

SCENE 3

On stage:	*No additional props required*
Off stage:	Playbill (**Barnum**)
Personal:	**Miss Fotherington**: handkerchief

SCENE 4

On stage:	*No additional props required*
Off stage:	Big oriental cushions (**Opium Sellers**) Hookah pipes (**Opium Sellers**)
Personal:	**Fix**: ring **Passepartout**: chopsticks

SCENE 5

On stage: Telescope for **Miss Fotherington**

SCENE 6

On stage: *No additional props required*

Off stage: Picture of elephant (**Passepartout**)
                Life-sized puppet elephant (**Clowns**)

SCENE 7

On stage: *No additional props required*

SCENE 8

On stage: Card table. *On it*: poker cards; money
                Piano

Off stage: Carpet-bag (**Fogg**)

Personal: **Hostess**: gun
                Passepartout: letter, pen; ring

SCENE 9

On stage: Luggage

Personal: **Bride**: veil, sign reading " Just arrived"
                Jesse James: gun
                James's Gang: guns

SCENE 10

On stage: *No additional props required*

Off stage: Little model train

SCENE 11

On stage: *No additional props required*

Off stage: Luggage including carpet-bag of money (**Fogg. Passepartout,
                Miss Fotherington, Aouda**)

Personal: **Detective**: notebook and pencil

SCENE 12

On stage: *No additional props required*

Off stage: Lanterns (**Wives**)
               Kitbags (**Sailors**)

SCENE 13

On stage: *No additional props required*

Off stage: Suitcases (**Passepartout**)

SCENE 14

On stage: Banner reading " Welcome back to Greenwich"

Off stage: Luggage (**Katy**)

Personal: **Miss Fotherington**: ring

Samuel French is grateful to Charles Vance, Vice- Chairman of the Theatre Advisory Council, for the following information regarding the Firearms (Amendment) Bill:

"The Firearms (Amendment) Bill does not affect blank-firing pistols which are not readily convertible (i.e. those which do not require a Firearms Certificate). Among the reasons against imposing restrictions on such items is their use in theatre, cinema and television as a 'safe' alternative to real guns."

"The general prohibition on the possession of real handguns will apply to those used for theatrical purposes. It would clearly be anomalous to prohibit the use of those items for target shooting, but permit their use for purposes where a fully-working gun is not needed. As handguns will become 'Section 5' prohibited weapons, they would fall under the same arrangements as at present apply to real machine guns. As you will know, there are companies which are authorized by the Secretary of State to supply such weapons for theatrical purposes."

The exemption under Section 12 of the Firearms Act 1968, where by actors can use firearms without themselves having a Firearms Certificate, will remain in force.

Regulations apply to the United Kingdom only. Producers in other countries should refer to appropriate legislation.

LIGHTING PLOT

Practical fittings required: star-cloth. Red lighting in trunk/trapdoor

ACT I, Scene 1

To open: General exterior lighting, rain about to fall

Cue 1	Final notes of overture; crack of thunder *Rain effect*	(Page 1)
Cue 2	**Crowd**: (*singing*) " ... in my place." *Bring up spotlight on* **Passepartout**	(Page 3)
Cue 3	The scene comes back to life *Fade spotlight on* **Passepartout**	(Page 4)
Cue 4	End of song *Black-out*	(Page 4)

ACT I, Scene 2

To open: Spotlight on **Fix**

| *Cue* 5 | **Fix** laughs nastily
Cut spotlight on **Fix**. *Bring up spotlight on suitcase* | (Page 4) |

ACT I, Scene 3

To open: Swing spotlight from suitcase to **Master of Ceremonies**

Cue 6	**MC**: " — Mademoiselle Katy O'Flathery." *Black-out*	(Page 5)
Cue 7	When **Katy** and **Girls** are in position *Bring up full interior lights*	(Page 5)
Cue 8	At the end of song *Black-out*	(Page 6)

ACT I, SCENE 4

To open: General interior lighting

Cue 9   **Passepartout**: (*singing*) "I love you!"   (Page 9)
              Black-out

ACT I, SCENE 5

To open: Darkness

Cue 10   Sound of railway station   (Page 10)
              Bring up lights

ACT I, SCENE 6

To open: Tightly focused lighting for **Queen Victoria** and **Disraeli**

Cue 11   **Queen Victoria**: " ... on Mr Fogg succeeding."   (Page 11)
              Begin widening lighting to full exterior state

ACT I, SCENE 7

To open: Bring up full exterior lighting

Cue 12   **Fogg** glares at **Passepartout**   (Page 13)
              Black-out. Then immediately bring lights up on
                 model balloon high above the set

Cue 13   **Fogg**: " ... Tunisia by suppertime."   (Page 13)
              Fade lighting on model balloon. Return to previous
                 lighting state

Cue 14   The umbrella clouds move to obscure the basket   (Page 13)
              Darken lighting

Cue 15   **Tour Guide**: " ... tour of the Acropolis?"   (Page 14)
              Lighting change

Cue 16   Sand dance music. **Katy** enters   (Page 14)
              Bring up spotlight on **Katy**

Cue 17   Cymbal crash   (Page 14)
              Shaft of light on suitcase; cut spotlight on **Katy** *immediately*

ACT I, Scene 8

To open: General interior lighting

Cue 18	At the end of the song *Black-out*	(Page 19)

ACT I, Scene 9

To open: General interior lighting

Cue 19	**Fix**: (*singing*) "Bang! Bang!Bang!" *Lighting change*	(Page 21)
Cue 20	**Fix**: (*singing*) "Gotcha!" *Black-out*	(Page 22)

ACT I, Scene 10

To open: General interior lighting

Cue 21	**Guard**: " ... very dangerous." *Black-out*	(Page 23)

ACT I, Scene 11

To open: General interior lighting

Cue 22	**Queen Victoria**: " ...wager may be doomed." *Black-out*	(Page 24)

ACT I, Scene 12

To open: General exterior lighting

Cue 23	At the end of the song *Lighting grows darker for* Scene 13	(Page 26)

ACT I, Scene 13

To open: Dark and oppressive lighting. Bring up red lighting in trapdoor/trunk

Cue 24	**Passepartout**: " Eugene! Eugene!" *Black-out, then bring up dim lighting for scene change*	(Page 28)

ACT I, SCENE 14

To open: When ready bring up interior lighting focusing on train

Cue 25   At the end of song   (Page 30)
              Black-out

ACT II, SCENE 1

To open: Lighting on **Holmes** and **Watson**

No cues

ACT II, SCENE 2

To open: General interior lighting

No cues

ACT II, SCENE 3

To open: General interior lighting

No cues

ACT II, SCENE 4

To open: The same; immediately following

Cue 26   A door at the back of the stage opens   (Page 36)
              Scary red light spills from open door

Cue 27   **Fix** (*singing*) "Come on, boy, let's blow."   (Page 36)
              Lighting change to indicate interior of opium den

Cue 28   **Fix** laughs nastily   (Page 38)
              Dim lighting for scene change. Bring up spotlight on suitcase

ACT II, SCENE 5

To open: General exterior lighting; star-cloth

Cue 28   **Aouda** " ... you ever get to Japan?"   (Page 45)
              Black-out

ACT II, SCENE 6

To open: Bright circus lighting

Cue 29	Sound effect of tremendous applause	(Page 46)
	Black-out	

ACT II, SCENE 7

To open: General interior lighting

No cues

ACT II, SCENE 8

To open: General interior lighting

Cue 30	**Passepartout** enters	(Page 48)
	Dim general lighting; bring up spotlight on **Passepartout**	
Cue 31	The saloon come to life	(Page 48)
	Cut spotlight on Passepartout; revert to previous state	
Cue 32	**Fogg** arrives at the card-table	(Page 48)
	Focus lighting on **Fogg**	
Cue 33	**Everyone**: " Whist?"	(Page 48)
	Dim general general lighting; bring up spotlight on **Passepartout**	
Cue 34	**Passepartout**: "'... reminds me of you.'"	(Page 49)
	Restore general interior lghting	
Cue 35	**Saloon Hostess**: "Just get out of here."	(Page 51)
	Black-out	

ACT II, SCENE 9

To open: Black-out

Cue 36	Blast of sound effects	(Page 51)
	Bring up lights	
Cue 37	**Aouda**: "Ladies, knickers off!"	(Page 57)
	Dim lighting	

ACT II, Scene 10

To open: Spotlight on **Queen Victoria** and **Disraeli**

Cue 38	**Queen Victoria** and **Disraeli** exit *Cut spotlights; bring up general lighting*	(Page 57)
Cue 39	**Dr Watson** and **Sherlock Holmes** exit *Lighting change*	(Page 58)
Cue 40	A model train passes over and set collapses *Bring up spotlight on* **Queen Victoria** *and* **Disraeli**	(Page 58)
Cue 41	**Disraeli** "... with sufficient speed!" *Cross-fade spotlight to* **Fogg**	(Page 58)
Cue 42	**Fogg** exits *Cross-fade spotlight to* **Queen Victoria** *and* **Disraeli**	(Page 59)
Cue 43	**Sherlock Holmes** and **Dr Watson** exit *Lighting change*	(Page 59)

ACT II, Scene 11

To open: General exterior lighting

Cue 44	**Passepartout** and **Fogg** are escorted off *Lighting change*	(Page 61)

ACT II, Scene 12

To open: Exterior lighting. Bring up star-cloth

Cue 45	**Aouda**: (*singing*) "Can never be the same." *Bring up spotlights on* **Fogg** *and* **Passepartout**	(Page 62)
Cue 46	The **Detective** exits *Fade lights on* **Fogg** *and* **Passepartout**. *Restore exterior lighting*	(Page 62)

ACT II, Scene 13

To open: The same. Immediately following

Cue 47	**Fix**: "Well, well, well." *Black-out*	(Page 65)

ACT II, SCENE 14

To open: General exterior lighting

Cue 48	At the end of the song	(Page 68)
	Black-out	
Cue 49	When ready	(Page 69)
	Bring up full lighting for cast bows	

.

EFFECTS PLOT

ACT I

Cue 14	**Passepartout**: " ... to be very proud of me." *Sound of a train arriving*	(Page 29)

ACT II

Cue 15	Door at the back of the set opens *Smoke spills out from the open door*	(Page 36)
Cue 16	At the end of the song and dance routine *Sound of tremendous applause*	(Page 45)
Cue 17	**Passepartout**: "... is in our dressing-room." *Sound effect of elephant trumpeting*	(Page 46)
Cue 18	**Passepartout**: "Come and say hallo, Eugene!" *Sound effect of elephant trumpeting*	(Page 46)
Cue 19	**Passepartout**: "... show business and diva elephants." *Sound of Eugene, the elephant trumpeting indignantly*	(Page 47)
Cue 20	To open SCENE 9 *Blast of train sound effects*	(Page 51)
Cue 21	**Passepartout**: " ' ... Why wait?'" *Sound of train leaving*	(Page 56)
Cue 22	The **Mean Bandit** exits. Silence. *Sound of whistling wind*	(Page 57)
Cue 23	**Sherlock Holmes**: " ... do the crossword." *Sound of a train screeching to a halt*	(Page 58)
Cue 24	**Disraeli**: " ... with sufficient speed!" *Sound of hammering and sawing*	(Page 58)
Cue 25	To open SCENE 11 *Train noises*	(Page 59)
Cue 26	**Aouda**: " ... she'd had a ring stolen?" *Sound of a train departing*	(Page 61)
Cue 27	**Aouda**: " ... heart beating inside me." *Christmas bells*	(Page 64)
Cue 28	Laughter from the crowd *A church clock chimes nine o'clock*	(Page 66)

MADE AND PRINTED IN GREAT BRITAIN BY
LATIMER TREND & COMPANY LTD PLYMOUTH
MADE IN ENGLAND